WHY THEY BEHAVE
LIKE RUSSIANS

WHY
THEY BEHAVE
LIKE RUSSIANS

By JOHN FISCHER

HARPER & BROTHERS
PUBLISHERS · NEW YORK · LONDON

For

G. C. F. and E. W. F.

TABLE OF CONTENTS

FOREWORD

THIS BOOK IS AN OUTGROWTH OF A STUDY OF RUSSIAN history and power relationships which began at Oxford in 1933. During my wartime service with the Board of Economic Warfare this interest became a professional preoccupation. It was one of my duties to help supervise a number of basic studies of the Soviet economy, and in the course of this work I had to examine a stream of intelligence reports on Russian economic affairs. The appraisal and analysis of this data did much to crystallize my thinking about the nature of the Communist state.

The book is not intended to be either a defense or a criticism of the Soviet system. Rather it is an attempt to estimate how that system is likely to behave under the pressure of a new and still unstable balance of power. As the reader will note, I am indebted to certain lines of thought developed by such politically-diverse writers as Nicholas Spykman, Walter Lippmann, John Scott, Lenin, Sir John Maynard, Paul Winterton, John D. Littlepage, Bernard Pares, and Frederick L. Schuman.

I am even more indebted to a number of officials—necessarily anonymous—with long experience in Russian affairs in the American and British diplomatic and intelligence services, who have contributed generously their counsel and judgment. In some cases they afforded me access to certain information which would not have been available through any other source.

The main thesis of the book, as set forth in Chapters XI and XII, was originally outlined in an article in *Harper's Magazine* in August 1945; three other chapters were published in *Harper's* in the early fall of 1946. Acknowledgement is also due to *Life* and the *New Yorker*, which have published some of this material in somewhat different form.

The on-the-ground material was gathered during an assignment of slightly more than two months with an UNRRA mission to the Ukraine in the spring of 1946. These impressions were supplemented by later investigations in Berlin, London, and Washington. Most of my time in Russia was spent at the mission's Kiev headquarters, with brief visits to Moscow, Kharkov, Dnepropetrovsk, Zaporozhe, Poltava, Kremenchug, and a number of small villages. The book is in no sense a report on the work of that mission; no UNRRA official bears any responsibility for it; indeed, some members of the mission may well disagree with some of the observations expressed.

Finally, I want to disclaim any pretension to being an "expert" on the Soviet Union. Like most students of that fascinating and enigmatic country, I have come to believe in Paul Winterton's rueful dictum: "There are no experts on Russia—only varying degrees of ignorance."

J. F.

WHY THEY BEHAVE
LIKE RUSSIANS

CHAPTER
ONE

THE SCARED MEN
IN THE KREMLIN

THE COLONEL IN THE ASTRAKHAN HAT STEPPED IN
front of our car just as it swung onto the narrow cobble-
paved ramp which leads from Mokhovaya Street to the
Forest Gate of the Kremlin. Three soldiers, carrying automatic rifles with bayonets fixed, moved out of the darkness
just behind him. They closed in, two on each side of the
car, before it slid to a stop on the damp stones. In the glare
of the headlights I caught a glimpse of the bright blue collar tabs, edged with red, which mark the crack Internal
Security Troops of the NKVD, the political police.

While his men inspected the inside of the auto, the
colonel reached for our four passes. He checked the numbers against a list in his notebook and held each of the little
tan cards up to the light to note its signature and distinctive
markings. Then he thumbed through our passports, read
every line of the Soviet visa in each of them, and compared
the photographs with our faces. Finally he handed back the
documents, saluted, and waved the car on. Nobody had
said a word.

Just before we reached the gate—a tunnel through a massive medieval tower of red sandstone—we passed another guard in a black-and-white-striped sentry box. Six more NKVD men with tommy guns stood just inside the gate. The car, moving fast now, shot by them into a great paved courtyard, bright with floodlights. It pulled up beside a high iron fence which stretched across the middle of the court. As we stepped out, four guards—all officers, armed with automatic pistols in polished leather holsters—again examined our documents with grave courtesy before they ushered us through the barrier.

In the minute or two which it took to walk across the inner court, we passed five riflemen. They stood at every door and passageway of the yellow stucco buildings which formed three sides of the enclosure. We headed for the largest of these buildings, the old Romanov palace which now serves as the assembly hall for the Supreme Soviet. Eight NKVD officers met us at the entrance. Their uniforms were immaculately tailored and none wore less than three medals. After a final careful scrutiny of passes, we were escorted through a maze of walnut-paneled anterooms and corridors to a little gallery overlooking the long hall where the Supreme Soviet—the Russian equivalent of Congress—was in session. Six plain-clothes men, looking like detectives the world over, lounged in the foyer which led to this gallery, and one of them accompanied us to our seats. He could hardly have regarded us—three American representatives of UNRRA with our interpreter—as dangerous characters; but he sat close behind us all the time we were there.

Below, in what was once the imperial court, sat some twelve hundred delegates who (according to the Soviet constitution) make up the ruling body of the USSR. Later I was told that very few of them had ever been admitted to any other room in the Kremlin. Nor did any of them carry briefcases here, although most Russian officials feel virtually naked without one.

They conducted their deliberations under the eyes of blue-uniformed guards stationed at six-foot intervals along the wall. ("Deliberation" is perhaps a misleading word. The delegates listened passively to the set speeches, and I am told that they always vote "yes" with machine-tooled precision. There was no debate from the floor, and there is no record that any delegate ever cast a dissenting vote.) Additional guards were posted at each door, and at the end of every aisle stood an alert officer of the NKVD. I have never seen any building, not even Eisenhower's wartime headquarters, so elaborately protected.

It seemed a fair conclusion that somebody in the Kremlin was scared.

For the next two months, as we traveled about western Russia, hardly a day passed that we did not encounter other signs of this pervading fear. The most obvious symptom, of course, was the Red Army—still mobilized four and a half million strong in spite of Russia's desperate need for manpower. Men in uniform were everywhere, often fully armed. It was by no means unusual for them to carry their rifles and tommy-guns in stores, markets, and even street cars. Military trucks (nearly half of them Lend-Lease Studebakers and jeeps) made up the bulk of the road traffic, and every airport was lined with long ranks of Yak and Stormovik fighter planes.

It showed, too, in many little incidents—the nervousness of a Russian official when our American interpreter wanted to carry her camera on a Sunday-afternoon outing; the unobtrusive little men in blue serge suits who kept turning up in the back of our box at the opera; the prison camp for Russian civilians just across the road from the Kharkov airport; the guard cars loaded with plainclothes men which trailed the limousines of most important Soviet bureaucrats. It was evident in the embarrassed refusals of nearly everyone whom we asked to our rooms for a chat and a cup of tea. The Ukrainians are the friendliest kind of people, but in the 1937 purge a good many Soviet citizens disappeared for no apparent reason except that they had once been on cordial terms with a foreigner—and the lesson has not been forgotten.

And in the background there was always the NKVD, beyond question the most efficient and most pampered organization in Russia. Its special army, including Border and Internal Security forces, probably numbers less than half a million men, but they are the best-trained, best-equipped, and most handsomely uniformed troops in the Soviet Union. Its secret police is at least two or three times as large. No foreigner really knows, but the estimates given me by a number of diplomats with long experience in Russia never ran to less than a million. Protection on this scale naturally does not come cheap. One report, which I believe to be reasonably accurate, placed the internal security budget for 1945 at 7,000,000,-

000 rubles or $1,400,000,000 at the official rate of exchange, but since such statistics are not made public in the Soviet Union, it is impossible to verify.

It seems curious that any government should feel the need for such lavish precautions—especially a government which has just crushed its only foreign enemies and apparently is popular with its own people. (In those parts of Russia where I worked, at any rate, I could find no evidence of serious disaffection. The Ukrainians—who make up a good fifth of the total Soviet population—sometimes grumble about a good many things, but most of them appeared honestly convinced that their government, for all its shortcomings, was the best in the world.)

Yet a sense of fear quite plainly is one of the dominating facts of postwar Russia. It is a fact of pointed interest to Americans, since it is shaping—or warping—the entire Soviet foreign policy. To the ordinary Russian it is even more pointed, since it is likely to condemn him to at least ten more years of the strain and sacrifice of a war economy.

Who is it, then, that is so scared? And why?

The first answer is not hard to guess. Like nearly every impulse of real importance in modern Russia, the national fear neurosis could spring from only one source—the group of fourteen men who boss the Soviet Union. They make up the Politburo, the directing brain of the Communist Party. They also hold the key jobs controlling every nerve-strand of the country's administration. Their lithographed portraits adorn millions of homes, schools, offices, and billboards. From their offices in the Kremlin—

the exact location is a carefully guarded secret—flow the orders which turn every wheel from the Danube to the Bering Straits. Their names are Stalin, Molotov, Beria, Malenkov, Zhdanov, Kaganovich, Voroshilov, Mikoyan, Andreyev, Khrushchev, Shvernik, Voznesensky, Bulganin, and Kasygin.

These fourteen work as a board of directors in almost daily session. In theory it has no chairman. In practice, of course, Stalin is the head man; but there are indications that he does not operate as a lone and arbitrary autocrat. For one thing, running Russia is not a one-man job. For another, the thirteen men who sit with him are nobody's stooges. They are tough, able, and aggressive characters, and each of them controls a considerable span of power in his own right.

Moreover, British and American officials who have had dealings with the Kremlin for the last seven years have noted certain sharp divisions of opinion within the Politburo. Four members, in particular, generally appear to act together. They form an inner circle of Stalin's most trusted lieutenants, and it probably is a safe bet that one of them will be his successor. They are:

1. Molotov, foreign minister and (to judge from the tone of the carefully modulated Russian press) Number Two in the party hierarchy.

2. Beria, a bald, suspicious, tight-lipped mountaineer—aside from Stalin the only Georgian on the Politburo. The apparatus of the secret police remains under his supervision, although the Ministries of Interior and State Security

recently were turned over to two of his aides. He also is in charge of the government's frantic efforts to develop atomic energy.

3. Malenkov, known among the smaller-fry bureaucrats as The Fat Boy. He once worked as The Generalissimo's personal secretary, and his card-file mind has become a Russian legend. Today, as one of the secretaries of the Party, he sits at the switchboard of the country's political machine. All important appointments, promotions, firings, and transfers pass through his hands. From a similar position twenty years ago, Stalin was able to outmaneuver all his rivals for power.

4. Zhdanov, another protégé of The Generalissimo and his troubleshooter in countless delicate political situations. He is the boss of Leningrad, a job comparable to the governorship of New York. He, Malenkov, and Stalin are the only men who sit on both the Politburo and the Party Organization Bureau, the next most important body in Russia.

These four gradually have become known as the extreme nationalists, the tough guys, the proponents of a vigorous policy abroad and a tight rein at home. On occasion their proposals have caused a good deal of misgiving among their colleagues, and Stalin himself apparently has stepped in from time to time to impose a "moderate" compromise. This kind of bellicose behavior is of course a common symptom of inner insecurity, and it may well be that of all the fourteen scared men, these four are the most frightened. There is even some reason to believe—as we

shall see—that one of them makes it his business to en-
gender a feeling of suspicion and uneasiness among his
associates.

What frightens them is not so easy to say. Some good-
hearted Americans seem convinced that it is merely the
atom bomb, and that if we were to hand over The Secret
all Russian misgivings would vanish overnight. Such an
answer surely is too simple; the guards at the Kremlin gate
aren't on watch for an atom bomb. No outsider, of course,
can do more than guess at what goes on in the mind of the
Kremlin. Yet the scant facts at hand seem to indicate that
the pattern of fear is a complex one, blended of at least
five separate elements.

One of these no doubt is sheer personal anxiety. The
men behind the red wall remember how they rose to
power, and they don't intend to leave that route open to
any other group of determined conspirators. They remember, too, that over the course of centuries an aston-
ishingly high percentage of Russia's rulers died by violence.
Most of all they remember the murder of Sergei Kirov.

When Kirov was shot to death in his Leningrad office,
one winter afternoon in 1934, he was Stalin's closest personal friend and heir apparent. He was killed by a Comrade Nicolaev, until that moment a trusted member of the
party. For sixteen years there had been no attempt to
assassinate a leader in the Bolshevik hierarchy; and all the
costly and sensitive antennae of the secret police had failed
to transmit any hint of danger.

For forty-eight hours after the shot was fired, Stalin
seemed to trust no one in Russia. He hurried to Leningrad

to question the murderer personally, and before he boarded his private train in Moscow every human being was cleared out of an area stretching nearly a mile around the station.

The investigation which followed dragged on for three years. It uncovered a conspiracy reaching into the very bowels of the Party, the Red Army, and the secret police itself. The resulting purge inevitably was tinged with panic; eventually there came an official admission that many innocents had suffered along with the guilty in the great wave of executions and imprisonments. Such crude and ruthless surgery—however justified by the politics of survival—could not help but leave scars and some itch for revenge. Is it any wonder, then, that members of the Politburo seldom appear in public, or that they prefer to drive behind panes of dark-tinted bulletproof glass? If Kirov wasn't safe, who is?

Another clue to Russian behavior lies in the geography of the country. Naked plains stretch both east and west with no barrier to provide a defensible frontier. These plains have served as open highways for invading armies—Mongol, Tartar, Polish, Swedish, French, and German—since the earliest record of Slavic history. Fourteen times since 1800 hostile troops have poured across the western border; Minsk has suffered precisely 101 foreign occupations; Kiev has been sacked so often that its citizens have lost count. And every invader since Genghis Khan has sent spies and fifth columnists ahead of his troops.

The result is a suspicion of foreigners, a secretiveness, an obsession with security which was fully developed centuries before the present regime. It was full blown in the

court of Ivan the Terrible, who set up a corps of political
police as early as 1564 and who eventually killed his own
son in a fit of suspicion (probably well founded). The ancient obsession was of course greatly intensified by the
shock of the last war. I have walked through cities such as
Poltava and Kremenchug where eighty per cent of all
buildings were razed, not in battle but by notably efficient
German demolition battalions. For two months I lived
within half an hour's walk of the Baba Yar ravine, where
one hundred and forty thousand bodies from the SS death
camps were dumped in layers and covered by bulldozers;
bones still wash up in every thunderstorm. I have talked to
a farmer whose wife and children (one of them seven years
old) were hanged because he fought with the Partisans,
and to nurses whose hospitals were soaked with gasoline
and burned with the patients screaming in their beds. These
are by no means isolated cases; nearly every family in the
Ukraine has its own story of German terror. If these people view the outside world with a certain nervous mistrust,
we may think it regrettable, but we shouldn't be surprised.

A third reason for the Politburo's misgivings is its aware-
ness of the country's enfeebled condition. A foreigner who
looks at the list of Russia's vast resources in land, manpower, and raw materials is likely to forget that—for the
moment—these add up to only *potential* strength. For all
its astonishing industrial progress in the thirteen years before the Nazi attack, the Soviet Union was still largely an
agricultural nation and a rather backward one at that. It
scraped through the war by the narrowest of margins—a
margin provided only by Hitler's bad judgment and Amer-

ican Lend-Lease. During the course of the struggle it lost a stunningly high proportion of its factories, homes, farm machinery, livestock, and skilled workmen. Soviet officials —including Nikita Khrushchev, a member of the Politburo and boss of the Ukraine—told me frankly that they could not be completely replaced for at least a decade. After looking at the tangled mountains of scrap metal which once were the industrial centers of Dnepropetrovsk, Kharkov, and Zaporozhe, I am convinced that their estimate is conservative.

Because of the Germans' methodical destruction of tools and equipment—even to wheelbarrows and farm carts— the pace of reconstruction is painfully slow. In all the Ukraine I saw only two wheelbarrows. (Even before the war they were not numerous.) For moving rubble and earth, laborers ordinarily use a sort of crude wooden tray, with handles at each end. Masons often carry bricks in their arms and slap on the mortar with their bare hands because they lack hods and trowels. Modern steam shovels and bulldozers are pitifully scarce. As a result, the rubble was still piled high on both sides of the main street in Kiev, capital of the Ukraine, nearly two years after its liberation.

Incidentally, nearly all the destruction was done by the Germans. I was surprised to find that neither the Soviet's famous scorched-earth policy nor its removal of factories to new sites beyond the Urals was carried out on anything like the scale which the outside world had been led to believe. The great Dnieper dam, for example, was only partly crippled when the Russians abandoned it; the power plant was untouched, and except for a relatively small center section the dam itself was left intact. The Germans soon had it repaired, although they were never able to put its electric current to much use. When they finally were forced back from the river, they razed the dam to its foundations and blew up all nine of the giant turbines. Similarly, most of the Ukraine's industrial plants, including its largest steel mill and the big Kharkov tractor factory, fell into German hands almost undamaged. The Russians succeeded in moving only the lighter machinery to the East; consequently the new wartime industrial centers in Siberia were built up, in the main, not from "refugee factories" but with American Lend-Lease equipment.

The most crippling loss of all was the destruction of the rail network throughout western Russia. Never adequate for a modern industrial nation, the transport system came out of the war literally in splinters. As a result the fast passenger express from Moscow to Kiev, for example, now feels its way over a hastily patched roadbed at an average speed of fifteen miles an hour. Every siding and junction is heaped with burned-out rolling stock, and an unbombed station is a curiosity. Passengers crowd the train roofs and corridors and—even in the coldest weather—hang in clusters on every step and coupling. Nor can the highway system take up the slack, because there is no such thing as a highway system. Cobbled roads radiate for only a few miles out of the larger cities. Beyond lie the dirt tracks, hub deep for three months in dust and clogged the rest of the year by snow and mud. Even our jeeps bogged down in that bottomless gumbo.

This near-paralysis of transport is clamping a powerful

brake on Russia's economic recovery. It cannot be fully cured until the steel mills of the Donbas are rebuilt, because huge tonnages of metal are needed for rails, bridges, and new rolling stock. But meanwhile reconstruction of the Donbas, once the industrial heart of the Soviet Union, is held up by lack of transport to move coal, iron ore, pit props, and machinery. Official statements published late in 1946 reported that both coal production and restoration of rail traffic were lagging far behind schedule.

From the military standpoint, this means that Russia is like a giant temporarily exhausted from loss of blood, with the severed arteries of his right arm still unhealed. Even if the atom bomb had never been invented, the Soviet Union today and for some years to come cannot begin to match the military and industrial potential of the United States. And to the men in the Kremlin this fact is profoundly alarming.

Americans find it hard to believe that anyone could regard us as a menace. Yet to every good Communist we are precisely that—a threat potentially more dangerous than Nazi Germany. In fact, since February 9, 1946, no loyal member of the Party has dared think of America in any other light; to do so would be heresy, punishable by excommunication or worse. For on that date Stalin himself set forth the doctrine that another war is virtually inevitable, and he implied unmistakably that the attack probably would come from the United States.

This notion is understandable only in the peculiar terms of modern Marxist theology. One of its basic articles of faith is the theory that the capitalist world can never escape from its fated cycle of booms and depressions, that each new depression is worse than the last, and that eventually the capitalist ruling class turns in desperation to fascism, imperialism, and aggressive war as the only way out of its economic troubles. "Thus," Stalin explained, "the first world war was the result of the first crisis of the capitalist system of world economy, and the second world war was the result of a second crisis."

A third crisis must be expected, because peaceable settlement of economic conflicts "is impossible . . . under present capitalist conditions of the development of world economy." Consequently the Soviet Union must embark at once upon a new series of Five Year Plans to raise its steel production to sixty million tons a year and its output of other war materials to comparable levels. "Only under such conditions," The Generalissimo warned, "can we consider that our homeland will be guaranteed against all possible accidents."

Such "accidents" obviously are expected to originate in the United States, since it is the citadel of capitalism and the only remaining nation capable of challenging the Soviet power. The moment of danger, the Communists believe, is likely to come in the decade after 1950, when they confidently expect America to sag into a catastrophic depression. According to Marxist doctrine, this almost certainly will result in a Hitlerlike dictatorship, which will then embark on a campaign of imperialist aggression. Therefore, even during the war, when Russia's proclaimed policy was co-operation (carefully limited) with its capitalist allies, Party executives both in the USSR and abroad were pri-

vately warned that this "friendship" was a purely temporary expedient—that there was no likelihood of lasting collaboration between the two worlds.

To the average Russian this warning seemed amply justified by Churchill's famous plan, voiced at Fulton, Missouri, for an Anglo-American alliance. The speech was
immediately denounced by Stalin as "a call to war against
the USSR," and the whole Soviet propaganda machine cut
loose with a barrage of vituperation against Churchill and
his "fascist friends in Britain and America." (The Russian
press as usual did not carry the text of the speech, but
only the official reply.) The result was a shiver of horror
through the entire country. Dozens of war-weary little
people—farmers, train porters, bookkeepers, who normally
took no interest in politics—asked me anxiously why these
evil men were trying to set the world aflame again. And
why didn't President Truman denounce these warmongers
as Stalin had?

From that time on the Russian press and radio began to
speak in an increasingly chilly voice about the United
States. (They had long been pouring a stream of hostile
criticism on Britain and its Socialist leaders, whom the
Communists regard as Marxist heretics even more wicked
than simon-pure capitalists.) Almost every day some item
appeared about America's "imperialist" efforts to set up
permanent military bases in Iceland and the Pacific, or the
pampering of "quisling war criminals" in American refugee camps in Germany. The tone was set by Professor
P. F. Yudin, a sort of court theologian and a revered authority on Marxist doctrine. He demanded a strengthening

of the Red Army because "the Soviet Union is surrounded
. . . by capitalist states which are constantly sending in a
stream of diversionists and spies."

How far this text has sunk into the minds of the Russian people was illustrated by one typical seven-year-old
schoolgirl. When an interpreter asked her what she wanted
to be when she grew up, she replied:

"A Red Army nurse and help fight the fascists who sur-
round our country."

She will be well prepared. Military training for both
boys and girls starts in the fourth grade of Soviet schools
and continues through college. Red Army instructors are
attached to each school, and we frequently saw ten-year-
olds drilling with wooden guns in play yards.

This Soviet apprehension, so deeply rooted both in
dogma and in Russian history, probably has been deliberately cultivated by the country's most potent bureaucrats,
the political police.

For a quarter of a century this organization under its
various names—the Cheka, OGPU, and NKVD—has enjoyed a highly privileged position. Its officials have been
entitled to the choicest food, clothes, cars, and ballerinas.
Its funds have been virtually unlimited, its equipment
the best the country can produce. (The Russian telephone system, for example, is chronically afflicted with
odd noises and unpredictable breakdowns, but the twenty-
one NKVD dictaphones which recently were found concealed in the baseboards of a foreign government's build-

ing in Moscow proved, when tested, to be of excellent quality.)

Above all, the police machine has enjoyed great power. It holds, quite literally, the power of life and death over anyone in Russia except Stalin himself. It can demand access at all times to files, safes, letters, bedrooms, and kitchen cupboards, with no nonsense about privacy. Its dossiers record the most intimate details of the lives of everybody of any consequence in the Soviet Union and of thousands of unsuspecting people abroad. (The NKVD operates its own espionage network, separate from that of the Red Army, in every quarter of the world.) Not even the Soviet elite, the officers of the Red Army and the Party, are beyond the reach of its dread hand.

This organization was founded to combat the foes of the Revolution, foreign and domestic. The domestic enemies —czarist nobles, capitalists, kulaks, and such dissident revolutionists as the Mensheviks—were soon disposed of, but the foreign enemies remained a very real threat. First there was the 1918 intervention of the frightened capitalist powers which hoped to strangle the Bolshevik regime in its infancy. After that had failed, there was always the threat of land-hungry Japan and, a little later, Nazi Germany. From the available evidence there can be no question, it seems to me, that Germany and its satellites did make a strenuous effort to plant spies and fifth columnists inside Russia, working with the Trotskyites and other disgruntled elements, and that the NKVD did perform an invaluable service in blocking these attempts. (The excesses which followed in the Great Purge are quite another matter. Any nation which employs an all-powerful secret police can take it for granted that such power eventually will be abused.)

With the end of World War II, however, the NKVD's chief reason for being simply evaporated. Every foreign enemy was crushed; at home the regime was wildly acclaimed by a grateful people. Consequently, the police bureaucracy had only two choices: it had to peel off its shiny uniforms, give up its power and privilege, and go out of business—or it had to discover a new threat. No country, not even Russia, would long tolerate such a costly and burdensome apparatus unless it seemed clearly indispensable.

Now it is not the nature of any bureaucracy—Russian, American, or Fiji—to go out of business voluntarily. The records of congressional appropriation hearings are full of the ingenious arguments for continued existence which any federal bureau can produce when its original job is finished. Prewar Persia provided a still more instructive parallel. Nearly every session of its parliament would produce a strong movement to cut the budget of the secret police. Then, just before the motion came to a vote, the police would discover a new plot on the life of the shah. Any legislator who voted for the budget cut would practically be voting for assassination, so the police appropriation always was approved unshorn. It would hardly be surprising, then, if much the same sort of thing began to happen in Moscow as the war drew to its close. If Beria and his lieutenants produced intelligence of fresh dangers, of plots for a new capitalist encirclement by Russia's former allies, they would simply be obeying the oldest instinct of politics, the passion of the functionary for his function. And a number of Western diplomats who have been working closely with the Russians believe that this is precisely what is happening.

Time and again negotiations over relatively minor issues have been disrupted by an upsurge of Russian suspicion—based apparently on sudden and ominous reports from the NKVD espionage apparatus. Rumors that America was forming a Yugoslav Royalist army in its zone of Germany, that OSS operatives were training Ukrainian refugees to serve as spies, that the British were maintaining a whole army corps of German prisoners with its formations intact and weapons stored close at hand—these and countless similar tales have kept Soviet officialdom in a constant dither of mistrust. By the time each of them is laboriously disproved, other rumors take their place.

Such stories, however improbable, carry weight in the Kremlin because members of the Politburo live in almost hermit isolation. Except for Molotov, they seldom have any direct contact with foreigners, or with anyone else except a tight circle of their own top officials. The NKVD is one of their three chief sources of information. The other two are the Party and the Soviet Foreign Office, in that order of importance. Unlike American bureaucrats they cannot check their official information against newspaper accounts, for the Russian press is not an independent newsgathering agency but rather a funnel for passing on whatever scraps of official information may be deemed suitable for public consumption.

The Communist Party, with its disciplined membership in every country, is of course a highly efficient intelligence organization. Both its reports and those of the Foreign Office, however, probably tend to confirm rather than to correct the distorted picture of the world which is drawn by the NKVD. These reports are drafted by men long trained in Marxist habits of thought, and their interpretations inevitably are colored to reflect the current Party line. Nor is such news coloring always unconscious; no prudent Communist would care to have his reports differ too widely from those of the secret police.

The danger of the Kremlin's dependence on such prefabricated information was well illustrated by the Finnish war of 1939. At that time the Soviet rulers appeared to believe quite sincerely that the Finnish workers and peasants were sympathetic to Communism and eager for liberation from a handful of capitalists and "Mannherheim White Guards." Consequently, there seemed no need for a major campaign; a few Red Army reserve divisions should be enough for the job. These troops, inadequately trained and equipped, marched across the border with bands playing. They had been ordered to expect a joyous welcome from the Finnish proletariat, who would quickly overthrow their oppressors. Actually the Finnish workers were waiting in the bushes with machine guns; the reserve divisions were butchered; and Russia found itself involved in a prolonged, bloody, and embarrassing campaign.

Perhaps the greatest danger to peace is the possibility that the Politburo will make another such error in its calculations about the outside world. For reasons noted later, I think it likely that the Soviet Union does not plan to start another major war itself—certainly not for the next twenty or thirty years. But there is always a chance that it may blunder into one as it strives—under the pressure of an almost neurotic fear—to build up a protective belt of satellite states outside its vulnerable borders.

In the following chapters I have tried to show how this fear of war is affecting the Russian people—their jobs, living standards, and personal freedom—and the direction in which it is pushing Soviet foreign policy. From these facts it may be possible to make some tentative guesses about our own problem, so exasperating and so crucial, of learning how to get along with the Russians.

CHAPTER
TWO

TEXANS
IN FUR HATS

THE UKRAINIANS ARE THE TEXANS OF RUSSIA. They believe they can fight, drink, ride, sing, and make love better than anybody else in the world, and if pressed will admit it. Their country, too, was a borderland—that's what "Ukraine" means—and like Texas it was originally settled by outlaws, horse thieves, land-hungry farmers, and people who hadn't made a go of it somewhere else. Some of these hard cases banded together, long ago, to raise hell and livestock. They called themselves Cossacks, and they would have felt right at home in any Western movie. Even today the Ukrainians cherish a wistful tradition of horsemanship, although most of them would feel as uncomfortable in a saddle as any Dallas banker. They still like to wear knee-high boots and big, furry hats, made of gray or black Persian lamb, which are the local equivalent of the Stetson.

The Ukrainians concede that their men and horses are bigger, their women a little prettier, than any others in Russia. They pride themselves on their freehanded hospitality, their easy friendliness, and they love to tell tall sto-

22

ries about Bogdan Khmelnitzky and Stepan Razin which sound remarkably like the legends of Sam Houston and Jesse James. They believe they won the war, with little help from the rest of Russia and none worth mentioning from the outside world. Nor is this conviction altogether unreasonable. One soldier out of every five in the Red Army was a Ukrainian, and their land was the great battlefield of the war; no other comparable area suffered anything like its devastation. Moreover, they heard very little about the fighting in western Europe and the Pacific, for the Soviet press never wasted much space on what it regarded as minor fronts. (They are sure the USSR was mainly responsible for the victory over Japan, too.)

Even the country looks a good deal like Texas—flat, dry prairie, shading off in the south to semidesert. Through the middle runs a strip of dark, rich soil, the Chernozom Belt, which is almost identical with the black waxy soil of central Texas. It grows the best wheat in the Soviet Union. The Ukraine is also famous for its cattle, sheep, and cotton, and—again like Texas—it has been in the throes of an industrial boom for the last twenty years. On all other people the Ukrainians look with a sort of kindly pity. They might have thought up for their own use the old western rule of etiquette: "Never ask a man where he comes from. If he's a Texan, he'll tell you; if he's not, don't embarrass him."

It was among these people that I spent most of my time in Russia, and since I was raised in Texas I felt at home from the beginning. Nowhere have I ever met more generous, kindly folk, nor any who behaved with such instinctive courtesy. Indeed, their hospitality was sometimes a little overwhelming, for they love to do things with a flourish. The morning we arrived in Kiev, for example—tired and bleary-eyed from a thirty-three-hour train ride—the delegation which met us in the station at 6 A.M. seemed unnecessarily cheery. They whisked us off to a five-course breakfast (beginning with vodka, caviar, smoked salmon, and dill pickles) and then plunged us immediately into a day-long tour of their capital, an expedition which they enjoyed immensely.

There were four in our mission, sent out by UNRRA to supervise the distribution of relief supplies throughout the Ukraine, an area larger than France and with about the same number of people. The chief was Marshall Mac-Duffie, a State Department officer and former lawyer. The others were Paul White, a Buffalo manufacturer, myself, and Mary Naimark, our interpreter and mainstay. She was a sunny, placid little woman who had migrated from Russia to the United States in her girlhood before the first World War and had been an American citizen for many years; few other people share her ability to speak both Russian and English with hardly a trace of accent in either tongue. Later the group was enlarged to a total of twelve Americans, two Englishmen, and one Canadian, some of whom stayed on until early 1947.

Before we came, the Soviet government had agreed that we should have complete freedom to travel throughout the Ukraine, talk to people through our own interpreter, and observe without obstruction what happened to UNRRA goods. This agreement was kept to the letter. We even moved about, whenever we chose, in our own automobiles which we shipped in for that purpose. The NKVD kept a watchful eye on us most of the time, as noted in later chapters, but did not attempt to interfere with our work.

Nobody, of course, can hope to learn much about a country in two months, even when he spends almost every waking moment traveling around, studying, and asking questions. Yet we had a chance to learn something about the Ukraine which, so far as I can discover, had not been afforded any other foreigner—whether journalist or diplomat—since 1933; and I think the opportunity was not altogether wasted.

The conclusions reported here are, of course, my own; other members of the mission might well disagree with many of them. Neither are they offered as expert opinion, for—as Paul Winterton has pointed out—there are no experts on Russia but only varying degrees of ignorance. I cannot even claim to be an unbiased observer, because all I saw and heard inevitably was colored by my own convictions and previous study of Russian history. The best I can do is to note those convictions—prejudices, maybe—and let each reader make his own allowance for them.

Briefly, then, I was raised as a Texas Democrat and expect to remain one. I have never been a Communist or a fellow-traveler and so have been spared the disillusionment which so often embitters disenchanted Marxists. I am convinced that the Communist political and economic system is completely unsuited—indeed, hardly conceivable—for the United States. On the other hand, I believe that some such system was inevitable for the Russians, in the light of their peculiar history and institutions. In any case, they are stuck with it; there is no prospect, so far as I can see, for any other kind of government in Russia within the predictable future. We could do nothing effective to change it, certainly, even if it were any of our business. Consequently, it seems clear we will have to make the best of the Russians as they are, and to learn to get along with them, somehow, in a swiftly shrinking world; for all of our lives depend on it.

For this reason, I have tried to record, as honestly and dispassionately as I can, how the Russians whom I knew were living, talking, and behaving in the disquieting spring of 1946. They are moved by worries, hopes, and habits which are strange to us but not altogether inexplicable. If we can learn to understand some of these things, or even to guess at their meaning, then perhaps Soviet behavior may not seem quite so frightening and difficult to deal with.

Many of the things we saw in the Ukraine are, of course, not typical of all the Soviet Union. Its living standards, for example, have been traditionally higher than anywhere else in Russia; the Ukrainian peasant eats more wheat bread than rye and hitches two horses to his cart instead of one. Because it lies on the western border and has been invaded with depressing frequency, the Ukraine is more westernized than most other sections of the country. It has its own culture and language—differing from Russian about as much as Scotch differs from English—which its people regard as obviously superior.

Its cities look quite different from those elsewhere in Russia. Many of them were rebuilt during the great wheat boom around the end of the last century, when wealthy landowners and merchants could afford to import the most fashionable Italian and French architects. As a result they were laid out·with broad streets, flanked by low houses stuccoed in pastel yellows, pinks, and blues, which produce a curiously Mediterranean atmosphere. At first glance, Kiev might almost be mistaken for Madrid, or Poltava for some town along the Riviera. Even in ruins they possess a sad, Italianate grace.

The buildings put up since the revolution did not seriously alter this character. Nearly all are either Packing Case Modern—the style favored for apartments—or Neo-Classic Grandiose. The Kiev headquarters of the Communist Party Central Committee, for instance, is a vast granite structure of the sort affected by bureaucrats everywhere, with an impressive but useless portico of Ionic pillars; it is about as revolutionary as an Iowa courthouse. Like most other public buildings, it was methodically gutted by the Nazi demolition experts before their retreat.

In other ways, too, the Ukrainians turned out to be surprisingly nonrevolutionary. Their morals, for one thing, would have delighted my old Methodist Sunday school teacher. Bawdy jokes are considered "uncultured" and are almost never heard in even the most robust company. The theater is decorous to the point of prissiness; even the ballet dancers wear knit-goods tights nearly as substantial as a flannel union suit. No cheesecake ever sullies a Ukrainian newspaper or magazine. Divorces are frowned upon and hard to get, while prostitution is punished by sentences of up to five years at hard labor. A normal amount of romance goes on in the parks of a summer night, but it is conducted with far more decorum than in, say, Central Park or Kensington Gardens.

Much of the current literature is pitched in the same stern, Cromwellian key. When Simonov, the popular author of *Days and Nights*, published a volume of moderately passionate love poems a few years ago, Stalin was said to have remarked that only two copies should have been printed—one for the writer and the other for the lady. Since then Simonov has stuck to the novel, specializing in heroic and inspirational themes. Of the foreign poets, one of the most respected is Longfellow; his conviction that life is real and life is earnest is widely shared by the Ukrainians.

Serious drinking is discouraged—except at formal banquets and similar affairs—both because it interferes with production and because it is considered unbecoming to citizens of the happy Workers' State. Vodka is sold for one ruble per thimbleful at sidewalk kiosks—that's the Russian word, too—along with sweet Caucasian wine and a violent pink soda pop. But there is nothing like the American juke joint or the British pub; the Soviet government does not encourage its subjects to sit around talking together except under the careful chaperonage of the Party. Consequently, it provides politically safe and wholesome recreation in the workers' clubs, which are attached to almost every office and factory. There the lower classes play chess, watch amateur theatricals, and listen to improving lectures on hygiene, city planning, and the theory of Marxism-Leninism.

Young blades who crave racier entertainment can take their dates—in Kiev, at least—to the ice-cream parlor in a little basement room on the city's main street. It was always crowded, and usually three or four giggling couples would be waiting on the steps for their turn at one of the twelve tables. There were restaurants, too, of course—just five, so far as I could discover, for a city of some six hundred thousand people—but only the more prosperous army officers and bureaucrats could afford to patronize them. The most popular was the dining room in the hotel where we lived, a rather barren hall with glaring lights and mustard-colored walls. There a couple could get salami sandwiches and a pitcher of beer for eighty rubles or about eight dollars in terms of American purchasing power. For a few weeks after we arrived a quite passable three-piece jazz band played there every night, but the manager eventually had to fire them because, he said, both the drummer and the trumpet player kept coming to work drunk.

For all their sober virtues, the Ukrainians are by no means a dour people. Their lives are bleak and hard, as we shall see in later chapters, but they have an astonishing vitality and capacity for enjoyment. This showed up most plainly on Sundays, when they would turn out for the *subotnik* or "voluntary" work on cleaning up the rubble of their battered cities. Every worker was expected to donate at least one Sunday a month to such work, but nobody regarded this as much of a hardship. Instead it was turned into a sort of community picnic. The whole family came along; wives set up tables on the sidewalk for tea and sand-wiches; the kids swarmed over the crumpled girders of the bombed-out buildings, playing the local variant of cops-and-robbers, known there as partisans-and-fascists. Often there was a sound truck, blaring out Cossack songs or such imported favorites as "Tea for Two" and "The Atchison, Topeka, and the Santa Fe." (Another current hit was "There's a Tavern in the Town," which the Rus-sians called "The American Soldier's Song." They be-lieved, for some unaccountable reason, that it was tre-mendously popular in the United States, and often sang it as a mark of respect whenever an American was present.) Nobody worked hard enough at the *subotnik* to get up a sweat, and there always was plenty of time out for long, passionate, arm-waving conversations. At the end of the day everybody rode home in army trucks, the boys sprawl-ing over the tail gate and the whole crowd roaring Ukrain-ian songs. For my money, they are the best singers in the world; they can harmonize, not just in four parts but in seven or eight.

And here, before we get on to more substantial matters, are a few random notes on how things were in the Ukraine:

Newborn babies are swaddled in king-size diapers which reach clear to the neck and keep their arms bound tightly to their sides. This is done, pediatricians told me, for psy-chological reasons. If a baby's hands were left untram-meled, he would wave them in front of his face, thus get-ting a fright which might permanently upset the nervous system.

Probably no children in the world get more affectionate care than Ukrainian youngsters. They are nearly all fat, sassy, and good-humored; very rarely did I hear one cry. It is not unusual for a mother to nurse her child well beyond his first birthday. If she works, as she almost always does, she gets time off to visit the local nursery at feeding time. Frequently mothers are able to pick up a little spare change by hiring out as wet nurses, after taking care of their own babies; their mammalian equipment can only be described as magnificent. Lana Turner wouldn't get a second glance in Kiev.

Of all the dozens of stores I visited, only one—a grocery in Kharkov—had an electric refrigerator, and I never saw any kind of refrigeration in private homes, nor a single refrigerator car on the railways. In the cities, as a consequence, fresh milk seemed to be a good deal scarcer than caviar.

All the Ukrainian traffic cops are women, dressed in snappy militia uniforms and armed with black-and-white-striped batons which they wave with elaborate grace. In Kiev, nine out of ten are blondes, and they are nearly all good-lookers. The rumor is that somebody high up in the police department personally selects the traffic details, with an eye to civic beautification.

Dogs are noticeably few in the Ukraine. The reason, I was told, was that they starved to death during the war, or were eaten by starving people.

There are no telephone books. They were all withdrawn as a security measure early in the war, and the government apparently does not plan to reissue them. Confidential directories are supplied to higher government officials only; each one is numbered and they are classified as secret documents. Information will not give you a number unless you can prove that you are entitled to it for official reasons. Consequently, when anyone making a phone call gets a wrong number—which is at least half the time—he usually asks what number it is and who is talking. By noting such information down over a period of months, he can gradually build up a private directory of his own. This is not so difficult as it sounds, because relatively few Russians have telephones.

Free enterprise has reared its persistent head all over the place. Anybody can go into business for himself, and many do. They cannot, however, hire (or, in the local terminology, "exploit") any labor. That means, in practice, that they can open such one-man enterprises as repair shops for alarm clocks, kitchenware, and shoes. These have become very common. In Kiev we passed street-corner cobblers' booths, usually made out of old packing cases, every few blocks. Some of these crates originally contained American aircraft and still bore Lend-Lease markings. Speculation also is a profitable—although somewhat disreputable and possibly dangerous—business, as we shall see in a later chapter.

Perhaps the nicest compliment the Ukrainians ever paid to the United States was in naming their dry-cleaning shops. They are called *amerikankas*, which might be translated as "The American Woman." The connotation is one of chic, neatness, and speed.

Stalin seems to be about the only man in Russia who

smokes a pipe. The usual smoke is a hand-rolled cigarette made out of a strip of newspaper and a pinch of *mahorka*, a violent variety of tobacco sometimes blended with sunflower leaves. Pipe tobacco can be bought, but almost never is, for about two dollars an ounce. The more prosperous smoke factory-made cigarettes with long cardboard mouthpieces, containing a mild, Turkish-flavored tobacco. Nobody smokes cigars, which have become a symbol of The Evil Capitalist, along with silk hats, bloated paunches, and spats.

The Soviet Frank Sinatra is a plump opera star named S. Y. Lemeshev, who has a pleasant tenor voice, big soulful eyes, and curly hair roached down over his coat collar like Senator Tom Connally's. His adolescent worshipers stop the show nearly every time he sings. I remember one performance of *Eugene Onegin* at which the girls in the audience ran down the aisles to the front of the theater and kept applauding until he made eight curtain calls. Some of them wore bobby-socks, too.

I was never able to buy bicarbonate of soda or any other indigestion remedy in a Soviet drugstore. No call for it, the clerks said; Russians just don't seem to be much bothered with stomach-aches. They use a lot of aspirin, though, usually mixed with caffeine, as a treatment for colds. It is considered strong medicine, properly taken only when the patient is in bed. Another popular treatment for colds is "cupping," a process for raising welts on the patient's chest and back by sucking the skin into a glass vacuum cup. The effect is much like that of a mustard plaster.

Kiev's most prominent civic improvement is a public-address system with loud-speakers rigged up on lamp posts and walls throughout the center of town. It broadcasted music and speeches most of the day, and sometimes far into the night. At 6 A.M. every morning it played a sort of municipal reveille, consisting of the first nine notes of "The Internationale" repeated over and over. The words which went with this scrap of music were: "Arise, ye prisoners of starvation."

CHAPTER
THREE

THE TIGHT BELT

FOR THE PAST THIRTY YEARS THE RUSSIAN PEOPLE have had a hard life. They are going to keep on having a hard life—by our standards, bitterly hard—for another ten or fifteen years.

That is a great deal to demand of anybody, even a people as durable and patient as the Russians. The handful of men who run the country are no doubt reluctant to ask it. They feel it can't be helped, however; for, as we have seen, they are convinced that another world war is almost sure to come. They expect it to be even more savage and exhausting than the last one, and they believe their nation must use all its energy and resources to get ready for it. In their eyes, another fifteen years of strain and sacrifice is the price which the Soviet Union must pay for survival.

Stalin broke the bad news to his people in his so-called Election Speech of February, 1946, which outlined the postwar course of the USSR. He told them then, with almost brutal honesty, that they had to set to work immediately on a new series of three or more Five Year Plans, directed primarily at building up a heavy industry (that is, a war industry) equal to any in the world. Until that is accomplished, he warned, the Soviet Union could not feel safe against another attack by its capitalist enemies. To drive the point home, he reminded them that he had been right when he had voiced a similar warning back in 1928 and had launched the country on the first of its famous Five Year Plans. At that time, he pointed out, "the Party knew that a war was looming, that the country could not be defended without heavy industry, that the development of heavy industry must be undertaken as soon as possible, that to be behind in this would mean to lose out."

At the cost of great hardship, the country did create a heavy industry; and it did not lose the war. It came out of the struggle almost exhausted, however, and with many of its painfully built factories in ruins. Now the Soviet leaders are convinced that the same kind of job—and more—must be tackled all over again.

Just how bad this news was did not dawn on the Russians until March 15, 1946, when the government announced the details of the first of its new Five Year Plans. This document outlined a truly backbreaking task. It called for the restoration of all industries wrecked in the war, plus an increase in output nearly fifty per cent above the prewar level. It sketched the design for a steel industry which eventually will turn out considerably more than the United States normally produces in peacetime. As a start, 104 rolling mills and 315 furnaces will have to be erected by 1950. Within the same period the railroads are to rebuild the 9,000 miles of track and 1,800 bridges destroyed by the Germans and complete 4,338 miles of new line. More than

7,500 locomotives and 472,000 freight cars must be put into service.

More important still, the Plan demands an increase in machine tools—the very heart of a war industry—up to a total of 1,300,000, which is thirty per cent more than all the machine tools America was using in 1940. The other essentials of a great industrial power—coal mines, turbines, refineries, chemical plants—all are to be expanded on a similar grandiose scale.

This blueprint of Russia's future makes no mention of atomic energy. Soviet spokesmen have repeatedly declared, however, that they expect to develop this, too, with all possible speed. Such an undertaking was by no means easy for the United States; for the USSR, with far less know-how in the chemical and electrical industries, it will be infinitely more difficult. Although Soviet scientists almost certainly have already worked out the basic "secret" of atomic fission, the construction of plants comparable to Oak Ridge and Hanford will absorb the cream of the nation's skilled labor for five to eight years. It also will swallow up a large share of the total output of such items as valves, pumps, high-quality alloys, and electrical apparatus, which are key components for many other industries.

Finally, the Red Army—the largest in the world—is to be re-equipped "with the newest armaments . . . in order to guarantee the country against all surprises." That will mean, to cite only one example, the creation of a virtually new aviation industry, since the Red air force has never had any modern long-range bombers and the best of its fighters now in operation already are obsolete.

All this adds up to one bleak fact: there won't be much left over for the Russian people. It simply is not physically possible for the country to achieve any considerable increase in its output of consumers' goods, on top of its huge program of capital investment. Indeed the Plan itself makes that fact quite plain. The tight belt will continue to be fashionable in Russia for a long time to come.

The Russian people know this, and they don't like it. They are accepting it, with some discreet grumbling, because most of them still have an almost religious faith in the wisdom of their leaders. (Those who don't—and I believe they are relatively few—either keep quiet or get sent off for a stretch of "re-education" in one of the political police's labor camps.) If Stalin says that another grueling period of sweat and privation is necessary—well, he knows best; but nobody else except the professional enthusiasts of the Party pretended to be overjoyed about it. Among the ordinary, sore-backed citizens, enthusiasm for the new Five Year Plan appeared to be very tepid indeed.

For these people are tired. Ever since 1914 they have been living under the tension of war or preparation for war. During the past six years, in particular, they have performed miracles of labor and self-sacrifice. Even now in western Russia they have to go on performing them simply to survive—entirely aside from the extra burden of the new industrialization program.

For example, when I met Maria Tretakova she had just finished building a house. She is sixty-three years old, and she built it with her own hands. Her tools were a spade, an ax, and a trowel. Her materials were clay, dug in her own back yard and mixed with straw into a kind of adobe brick, plus a cartload of lumber which she picked out of the rubble heaps along her street. For the roof, the local secretary of the Communist Party helped her get a few strips of tar paper.

It is a good house, as such things are measured these days in the Ukraine. It stands on the east bank of the Dnieper River, among the ruins of what was once the main industrial suburb of Dnepropetrovsk. When the Germans retreated, they blew up its forty-one factories and burned all but four hundred of its ten thousand homes. Like most of her neighbors, Maria had to live in a dugout for nearly a year, while she put up new walls on the charred foundations of her old cottage.

The new place has two rooms, each about ten feet square, and a little storm porch outside the door. When I was there, this porch also served as a woodshed, tool house, and shelter for the family pig, which was penned into one corner with two planks. The furnishings were a brick stove, built into the partition between the rooms, a homemade wooden chest, a stool, and an iron bed which Maria had dug out of the ashes of the district hospital. A gunnysack was spread beside the bed. On the walls hung an icon—a bright lithograph of the Virgin and Child, with a gilt frame—and a clock which her son had brought back from Germany. Five pegs in the wall held the family's spare clothes. There was nothing else—no mirror, no washbasin, no plumbing, no books, no curtains, not even a chair.

Vassily, the son who got out of the Red Army about the time the house was finished, told me that he hoped to build a table and perhaps a chair if he could find enough wood. Another bed won't be necessary; he sleeps on the stove, and the present bed is big enough for Maria and her daughter, who recently came home from a war factory beyond the Urals. The other two sons won't be coming home.

Maria had whitewashed the walls, inside and out, and still had enough lime left over for one coat on the privy at the far end of her little garden. She kept the packed clay floor swept clean with a twig broom. Her kitchenware—a brass teapot and two large tin cans (relics of Lend-Lease) —was polished to a high shine. Like most Ukrainian women, she naturally is a tidy housekeeper. Moreover, in the last twenty years she has been taught a good deal about "Soviet culture," which mostly means hygiene.

Keeping the place clean was quite a chore, however, because there was no soap. In theory, Maria was entitled to buy a hundred grams—one small cake—of laundry soap each month, but at the time I visited her the local stores had not been able to meet this ration for the past three months. She boiled her laundry with a little soda, when she could get it, or scrubbed it with a special kind of brown clay from the banks of the Dnieper, which is supposed to have some cleansing properties. It must have, because her clothes—a woolen head shawl, blue-striped cotton shirt, and worn black serge skirt—were fresh enough. She doesn't have to worry about stockings. In summer she goes barefoot; in winter she wraps her feet with strips of cloth and shoves them into knee-high felt boots.

In place of bath soap, the Tretakova household used the same brown clay—which was on sale for a few kopeks a pound in nearly all Ukrainian markets—or a mixture of wood ashes with a little sand. (Families with children usually prefer the clay; the ash-and-sand mixture cleans better, but it is a little rough on the babies' skin.) Occasionally American toilet soap turns up in the street-corner markets —the merchant seamen touching at Odessa trade it for vodka and souvenirs—but it brings as high as eighty-five rubles a cake, which is nearly as much as Vassily can earn in a week.

From the standpoint of privacy, the Tretakova family was better off than most of the Ukraine's city dwellers. In Kiev, least damaged of the big cities, each person was supposed to have six square meters of living space. That means a strip of floor about ten feet long and six feet wide—somewhat larger than a grave—on which to sleep, cook, eat, and store one's possessions. In Kharkov, which lost thirty per cent of its dwellings in the four separate battles for the city, the official allocation was 4.8 square meters. Even these space allotments could not always be met in full, as the thousands of refugees streamed back to their half-ruined towns.

The result is an overcrowding which the average American can hardly imagine. If you really want to know how a typical Ukrainian family lives, pick the smallest room in your house or apartment and move your wife and children into it. Then pack in the beds, spare clothes, and furniture which you regard as absolutely indispensable. Knock off a few chunks of plaster and most of the paint, to simulate the effect of fifteen years of undermaintenance. Scrap the radiators and cooking range and substitute for both a brick stove which seldom raises the winter temperature much above freezing. Break off the hot-water tap in the bathroom, which you will share with several other families. Finally, invite your widowed Cousin Sophie and her four youngsters to move in with you for an indefinite period. If things seem a little cramped, console yourself by reflecting that you are still better off than many Russians. I've known cases of four Ukrainian families sharing a single room. That, as one minor Kiev official expressed it, "doesn't make for friendship, or even for decent living."

Even before the war the housing shortage had been bad enough; 150 square feet for each person was the best ever achieved in any Ukrainian city, and the average was considerably lower. Now it is causing more discontent, so far as I could judge, than any other single hardship. The authorities were frankly worried. Nikita Khrushchev, the political boss of the Ukraine, kept an assortment of tiles, plywood strips, cinder blocks, and similar building-material samples spread out on a table in his office, and he fretted constantly about UNRRA's slow delivery of construction equipment. In the end I came to suspect that lack of homes, together with food shortages, might be one of the main reasons for the Kremlin's reluctance to bring its troops back from the occupied countries.

"When the soldiers come home," explained one of my friends, a Party member in a job of considerable responsibility, "they aren't in any mood to be patient and under-standing. They've been sleeping in snow and mud for five years, and they won't even listen to explanations about our construction plans for next year. They just say: 'We saved you from the Nazis—now give us some place to live.' When they have to wait, they get restless and some of them become demoralized."

Presumably it was one of these demoralized young men whom my interpreter and I met one night while we were strolling through the quiet streets to the south of Kiev's central market. (We went walking nearly every night, and if we ever were followed byNKVD plain-clothes men, I was not able to detect it. Nor did anyone ever try to prevent us from talking to people on the streets.) We stopped this boy to ask our way, and he walked with us for a few blocks because, he said, "maybe you can tell me how things are in other countries." Also he obviously was eager to tell somebody how things were with him.

Like many Red Army veterans, he was still wearing his uniform with the shoulder boards and insignia removed. Both of his boots were split open at the toes and he had no hat. His father, a colonel, had been killed, he said, and he himself had been twice wounded. He was not interested in any of the jobs he could find in Kiev—"they barely pay enough for bread"—and he had no home.

"I sleep where I can," he told us. "One night in the rail-way station; maybe on the floor of a friend's apartment the next. But there are thousands here who are no better off.

I guess I ought to hop a freight train to Odessa. I have relatives there who may be willing to give me a place to live. Anyhow, it's warmer than Kiev."

Such foot-loose, maladjusted veterans probably are largely responsible for the postwar crime wave which has plagued Russia as well as the capitalist countries. A whole division of cavalry had to be called into Moscow in the winter of 1945 to help the police put down an epidemic of robberies, and in Kiev I was repeatedly awakened in the night by the crack of rifle and pistol shots in the streets. How much of this nocturnal gunfire came from the police and how much from trigger-happy soldiers on a spree I was never able to determine. It was never mentioned in the papers, since crime—along with such other trivia as fires, automobile accidents, divorces, and weddings—is not considered news in Russia.

Hunger, too, was causing a good deal of open grumbling in the Ukraine. Nobody was actually starving while I was there; few people even looked thin. Ukrainian women, especially, are often downright buxom. Nevertheless, their diet is meager, unappetizing, and monotonous, even by prewar Russian standards.

If you were a Soviet housewife, you would start your shopping early, both to be sure of getting some food before the store sold out and because you wouldn't want to get your pay docked for being late to work. (Nearly all Russian women work, of course, since it usually is impossible to raise a family on the husband's pay alone, even though such items as rent and medical care cost little or nothing. The present wage of industrial workers in the Ukraine, as nearly as I could estimate, averages about 300 to 350 rubles a month—roughly $30 to $35 in terms of American purchasing power. The new Five Year Plan aims to raise the average to 500 rubles by 1950. Nor do the women always work at the genteel indoor jobs which are favored by the less robust, emancipated females of the capitalist world. They are widely employed in such trades as bricklaying, grading roads, and shoveling concrete on construction projects. The first gang of Soviet women I saw at work was clearing four inches of packed ice and snow off the Moscow streets. Though the temperature was well below freezing, they were breaking up the ice with crowbars and tossing the chunks into trucks with their bare hands.)

You would find that shopping in Russia is much simpler than elsewhere because you could buy your rations only at the one store where your ration card was registered, along with that of some two thousand other customers living in the neighborhood. Moreover, you could be confident that your store—in this case, let us say, Grocery No. 69 on Pushkin Street in Kiev—would have almost precisely the same stock as all the rest of the city's three hundred ration stores. Except, of course, those shops reserved for the privileged classes—army officers, scientists, teachers, doctors, pregnant women, and important bureaucrats—which have a somewhat wider selection of goods.

At this particular store, which looks much like all the others, you would find the show window nearly filled with a neat pyramid of American powdered-milk cans from a recent UNRRA shipment. On top of the pyramid stands a bottle of Crimean champagne, its label a bit fly specked and faded, since it has been used as a window decoration for many months. It costs as much as you can earn in a couple of weeks, and naturally the turnover in such delicacies is rather slow. A colored portrait of Stalin, edged with ruffled crepe paper, leans against the milk cans. It is surrounded by hams, cheeses, and slabs of bacon, all made out of plaster of Paris; their purpose is purely decorative, since such items have long been out of stock.

As you step through the door, you find yourself in a small room lined on three sides with shelves. Wooden counters in front of these shelves and a cashier's booth are the only furniture. The store is lighted by a single, unshaded forty-watt bulb, and its walls are decorated with large lithographed portraits of Stalin, Molotov, and Mikoyan, the minister of foreign trade. Its staff consists of the manager, a cheerful, stolid middle-aged woman, and four girl clerks. They are all dressed in head shawls, black leather boots, and white jackets like a doctor's uniform. These jackets are clean, because the regulations demand that they be washed every night, and the shop is tidy and well swept. (At any minute an inspector from the Trade Ministry may drop in to make sure these rules are being strictly followed.) The brightest of the girls sits in the cashier's booth, equipped with an abacus, the Oriental adding machine, and a money box made out of an old U. S. Army K-ration container. The store is crowded with other customers, but there isn't likely to be a queue except on the first days of the month when new ration coupons become good.

All the shelves along one wall are filled with square, unwrapped loaves of black rye bread, weighing just over two pounds each and priced at ninety kopeks or about nine cents. There also are a few loaves of whole-wheat bread, which sell for twice as much. The rest of the shelves are almost empty, although a few packages of Caucasian tea and a small assortment of U. S. Army rations and powdered-milk cans are spread out to make as brave a show as possible. Aside from the tea, all these items have been supplied by UNRRA, which bought them from American army surpluses. In one corner stands a barrel of sauerkraut, and on the counter is a two-gallon can of peanut butter— also with a U. S. quartermaster label—covered with an old copy of *Pravda* to keep out the flies.

You can buy nearly a loaf and a half of bread for the day—eight hundred grams for yourself, since you are a "heavy worker" on a railway bridge gang, plus six hundred for your husband who has a "light" job on the large bookkeeping staff of the State Planning Commission. You also are entitled to a weekly ration of about a pound and a half of meat and a pound of butter or lard; but you know the store hasn't had any of these for a long time, so as substitutes you get a can of powdered milk and half of an army Ten-in-One ration instead. Finally you buy a few ounces of peanut butter, wrapped in a scrap of paper, and a quart of sauerkraut ladled into the tin can you brought along for this purpose. All of this goes into the string net shopping bag which Russian women habitually carry.

Your dinner tonight, then, will consist mainly of black bread and sauerkraut soup, just like every other dinner for weeks past. If you are an especially ambitious (or hungry) housewife, however, you will stop by the open-air market on your way home from work in hopes of picking up a little extra to piece out your rations.

The market is simply two long rows of plank tables set up in the middle of a cobble-paved square just off the Khreshchatik, Kiev's Main Street. Farm women are lined up behind the tables, each of them with a few bits of food spread out on a handkerchief or newspaper in front of her. This is their surplus from the little garden plots, usually about an acre, which are assigned to every family on a collective farm. Whatever the family can raise on its privately held strip, it is free to eat, sell, or barter in good capitalist fashion. After she feeds her own household, a thrifty farm wife usually manages to save up something to bring to market once or twice a week—perhaps four eggs, a six-inch hunk of hard sausage, a crock of cucumber pickles, a raw pig's liver, a vodka bottle full of sour milk, a handful of sunflower seed, or a string of garlic.

Whatever it is will fetch a good price, because there are no price ceilings. Although it is perfectly legal, this bazaar is the economic equivalent of a black market. It sops up surplus purchasing power and provides an outlet for goods that are too scarce for successful rationing. Aside from the relatively small UNRRA shipments, it is the city dweller's only source of meats and fats. (There also are a few Gastronoms or "commercial stores," where the government itself sells such delicacies as caviar and canned crab

meat, but their prices are far beyond the reach of the average citizen.) Since the total supply of all kinds of fats—
mostly sunflower and linseed oil—averages less than a
pound a month per person and since meat is even more
scarce, the farm women have no trouble in getting twenty
rubles for a tenth of a pound of wurst or fifty rubles for a
chicken. Even for a medium-sized carp out of the Dnieper
River you would have to pay thirty-five rubles or the
equivalent of three and a half dollars.

But rubles don't interest the Russians nearly as much as
barter. As you shoulder your way through the market,
you will find that those American canned foods in your
Ten-in-One ration box, or the hard candies, or the envelope
of instant coffee will prove your best currency. The chewing gum—which they call "chewing rubber"—baffles the
farm women. It doesn't seem very nourishing, and they
can't understand why it should be in a military ration; but
somebody may swap an egg for a stick of peppermint, just
out of curiosity. The little packet of citric acid crystals is
practically worthless—one point on which Russians and
the American soldier apparently agree. You can, however,
trade off the cardboard ration box, its oiled paper lining,
and any empty bottles or tin cans you may have on hand.
All these things have a well-established market value in the
Ukraine.

What the farm women want most, though, is clothes.
Most of them are wearing the patched remnants of the
dresses which have seen them clear through the war. Some
don't even have a dress left. Many a strapping Cossack girl
comes to market in a quilted canvas overcoat, buttoned

tight over a threadbare cotton undershirt, and a pair of homemade birchbark sandals. If you can spare an old sweater or a printed rayon scarf which some soldier relative has sent back from Germany, you can trade it for a whole basketful of food or up to two hundred rubles in cash. That apparently was what one old woman had in mind when she described this market to me as "the place of miracles."

"I earn three hundred rubles a month," she said, "and it costs me twice that to keep my family alive."

She was miraculously closing the gap—temporarily— by selling off her wardrobe a piece at a time. And she added: "We are tired of these hardships."

It was a phrase I heard many times.

The government hears it, too, through the Party officials who serve as its eyes and ears in every village, office, and factory. The men in the Kremlin are quite aware of the weariness, the discontent, and the universal craving for consumers' goods. They also are aware that this discontent is not politically dangerous—at least not yet. The tone of the grumbling is louder but not much different from that of American consumers who are fed up with food shortages and house hunting; it is not the kind of noise which foreshadows open rebellion.

It does, however, indicate a lethargy, a flagging morale which could slow up considerably the tremendous undertakings of the new Five Year Plan. If it went unchecked, it might conceivably grow into another spasm of that sullen passive resistance which is the characteristic weapon of

Slavic peasant peoples and which so nearly wrecked the Bolsheviks' plans in 1920 and again in 1933.

Here, then, is the government's main internal problem: how to keep the tired horse pulling for another ten years on the thinnest possible feed of oats. Nearly everything that is happening inside Russia grows out of this problem and the Party's efforts to find an answer.

One obvious answer, of course, is to show the horse why he can't have more oats. Another is to persuade him that he is getting quite a lot already, and that a whole bagful is waiting just over the next hill. The Party is trying them both.

The first of these tactics, no doubt, is largely responsible for the increasingly fearsome picture of America which is being painted by the Soviet press. Unless the Russian people can be convinced that war is a real and immediate peril, they can hardly be reconciled to giving up the good things of life in order to build a great defense industry. Consequently, they must be told that the United States—obviously the only nation capable of tackling Russia—is becoming dangerously belligerent. Hence the familiar charges in the Russian newspapers that American "reactionaries" are developing atomic energy "not for the good of mankind but to its detriment as an instrument for oppressing and enslaving other peoples," and that the Good Neighbor policy is an imperialistic scheme for welding a "dangerous . . . military and political bloc" in Latin America.

These frightened noises do not necessarily reflect the real views of the Soviet government. Its fears of the United States are actual enough, but they are long range rather than immediate. It realizes that, for the present at least, American public opinion would never tolerate the use of the atomic bomb in an aggressive war, and that our shrunken army is no longer a serious striking force. The rude language of the Russian press, therefore, may be taken as a rough measure of the Kremlin's troubles at home. If they grow worse, the whooping about the American bogeyman is likely to get just that much louder. We shouldn't take this name calling too seriously; it is intended almost entirely for internal consumption.

At the same time, the government is trying hard to make the best possible showing with the thin trickle of consumers' goods which it is able to provide. In spite of some favoritism to the wealthy and privileged classes, the distribution of food and clothing is reasonably fair. It is also efficient. One UNRRA shipment of sardines was on sale in retail stores throughout the Ukraine only twelve days after it had landed in Odessa—fast work in any country, and little short of miraculous in an area where the railroads are still half crippled.

The importance of these UNRRA goods and of whatever imports the Soviets can wring out of the occupied countries is indicated by the extreme lengths to which the government has gone in order to get them. In the case of UNRRA, it made an unprecedented concession. It agreed to let a group of foreign inspectors travel freely throughout western Russia to watch the distribution of UNRRA supplies, simply because it could not get them on any other terms. In the occupied countries it has risked cutting its own political throat by its ruthless seizure of "reparations."

To the Russians, "reparations" apparently mean any enemy goods they can lay hands on, from an ice-cream factory to German bicycles, radios, wine glasses, sewing machines, cattle, and goose-feather pillows. All these items, and many more, were flowing into the Ukraine in a considerable stream while I was there. This process clearly is bad politics, since it must be hard to convince a Rumanian or Austrian family of the glories of Communism while Red Army men are hauling its furniture out of the house. But it can hardly be called unjust. Even if the Red Army stripped Germany and its satellites bone-naked, it could never make up for all they stole and destroyed within Russia.

Perhaps most significant of all is the fact that in their zone of Germany the Russians have built up certain industries—notably gasoline, synthetic rubber, and optical goods—to an output considerably above the prewar level. In theory, the USSR is committed to razing Germany's war industry; but for the moment it needs the finished products too urgently to bother about such theories, or about the suspicious protests of the other occupying powers.

The Soviet propaganda machine is making spectacular efforts to cover up the nation's shortcomings in consumers' goods, to persuade the people that they are well off in comparison with the capitalist world, and to assure them that real abundance is just around the corner. It is not always successful.

For example, I was never able to discover a single item in the Russian press—even with the help of Soviet librarians

—which gave UNRRA adequate credit for the two hundred and fifty million dollars' worth of food, clothing, and equipment which it was pouring into the country. Eventually, at the request of the mission, some accounts of UNRRA's contribution were published in the Ukrainian press, and occasionally the mission's activities were covered by local papers, radio, and newsreels. It was always obvious, however, that the government was reluctant to admit it needed outside help to feed its people.

Yet the Ukrainians knew very well where their UNRRA food was coming from, simply because they saw American labels on every can and K-ration box. Moreover, they were obviously grateful. Time after time UNRRA representatives were stopped in the streets or stores by some shopper who asked that her thanks be passed on "to our friends, the American people." Indeed, the United States got more than its fair share of credit for UNRRA supplies, since goods from most other countries —such as Indian tea, West African cocoa beans, and Australian blankets—were shipped in bulk, and their source could not readily be identified on the store shelves. Consequently, most Russians thought UNRRA was a purely American organization. (It might be overoptimistic, however, to conclude that the resulting good will has any great practical value. I was unable to find any evidence that the views of the ordinary Soviet citizen had the slightest effect on the Kremlin's foreign policy.)

Similarly, the press insistently assures the Russians that they are the happiest people on earth. As Paul Winterton, one of the most careful students of Soviet life, has expressed it, they have been "deliberately hoodwinked" into believing "that in the wretched bourgeois states all but a privileged few live in miserable conditions of unemployment and poverty." Nearly all news of America, for example, is carefully selected to give an unrelieved picture of strikes, racial persecution, and merciless exploitation of the toiling masses. The geography textbook used in all Soviet schools flatly states that "the huge wealth" of the United States "is in the hands of a small bunch of millionaires who . . . lead luxurious lives and sweat the workers as hard as they can. A working day lasts nine to ten hours. . . . At the age of forty-five, a worker loses his health and becomes an old man. . . . Agriculture also is in decay. . . . Many farmers have been pauperized and have abandoned their farms."

As a result of such propaganda, one relatively well-informed Communist was frankly incredulous when I told him that during the war OPA had been pretty successful in protecting tenants against unlimited rent increases, and another refused to believe that Negroes were permitted to attend American public schools. The few current American books translated into Russian are chosen to back up this impression. John Steinbeck, Sinclair Lewis, Theodore Dreiser, and Upton Sinclair are almost the only modern American writers who are widely known in the USSR, and the reader naturally concludes that the United States is peopled almost entirely by Babbitts and Okies.

Nevertheless, some doubts manage to creep in. Whenever a Russian looks at a Dodge or Studebaker Lend-Lease truck, he can't help but see that it is better than anything coming out of Soviet factories. Moreover, he looks at them often, since they make up nearly half of the road transport, and he may wonder how a "decadent" country manages to build such a lot of undecadent trucks. In addition, a surprising number of Russian soldiers met American troops somewhere along the Elbe or in Czechoslovakia and found that they did not look quite like downtrodden proletarians.

The worst leakage of all occurred when the Red Army moved into Germany and the Balkans. The troops then discovered that even in fascist countries almost everything from plumbing to women's underwear was more luxurious than anything they had ever seen. The result was a pop-eyed hankering for the fleshpots which all the efforts of Soviet propaganda have not been able to counteract entirely. The Red Army desertion rate in the occupied areas has been enormously higher than that of the American, British, and French armies.

All this makes it doubly necessary for the government to convince its people that their own supply of consumers' goods is increasing rapidly, and that if they will only be patient a little longer everybody will have an abundance. Nearly every Soviet newspaper is heavily larded with articles about the rising production of boots, textiles, and furniture, and with schemes for still further increases under the Five Year Plan.

Some of these gains are tangible enough. At this writing, bread rationing is expected to end sometime in 1947. (Meats and fats must stay under ration for a long while, since war-devastated livestock herds cannot be rebuilt in a year or two.) Such luxuries as buttons, safety pins, lipstick, and costume jewelry stamped out of colored plastic are becoming less rare. The commercial stores, where goods are sold without ration tickets, cut their prices last summer about forty per cent. A pair of men's shoes can now be bought for $81, for the cheapest grade, or $160 for the best. Silk stockings cost $12 a pair, men's suits range from $160 to $400, and gingham dresses sell for as little as $30. Moreover, similar items sometimes are available at the ration stores, in very limited quantities, at still more reasonable prices.

In one material respect—and, so far as I could discover, only one—the Soviet worker actually is better off than he would be in America. He gets medical and dental care absolutely free any time he needs it. The quality of treatment may not be first class, since Russian doctors get less schooling than their American counterparts, and wherever the Germans penetrated, the supply of drugs and equipment is still sadly short. If you went to the Kremenchug hospital, for instance, you would have to bring your own bedclothes, you would find the X-ray laboratory still in ruins, and your surgeon might have to wait his turn for a pair of rubber gloves.

Yet all the doctors I met impressed me as earnest, intelligent, and enthusiastic, and there were plenty of them, even in rural areas. Most villages—in contrast with American small towns—have some kind of hospital or maternity home. As a result, the peasant undoubtedly gets more medical attention than the average American farmer, and he never has to worry about being bankrupted by some unexpected illness. Perhaps it is not altogether accurate, however, to describe medical care strictly as a service for consumers. In the eyes of the government, manpower is primarily an element of military strength, and keeping it healthy is a matter of high military priority, much like the maintenance of tanks.

At first glance, the Five Year Plan's targets for consumers' goods look quite impressive. Farm production is to be increased 27 per cent; the number of automobiles in service will be doubled by 1950; 85 million square meters of living space will be built or repaired; and the total volume of retail trade is to rise 28 per cent above the prewar level. Through the rosy lenses of the Soviet press, this looks like an impending avalanche of everything a man could want.

A closer examination of the Plan, however, leads to more somber conclusions. The planned increases do not mean a clear gain in production but in large part merely reflect the expansion of the USSR, which has added territories containing 25 million people since the last Plan. The housing program will provide considerably less than one square yard of additional living space for each Russian citizen—a scant relief for the present overcrowding. A doubling of the number of automobiles will give the USSR a total stock which is only a fraction of Detroit's output in a single year, and virtually all of that must be allocated to the bureaucracy, the trucking services, and the army. Private cars will continue to be almost unknown. Even by 1950 shoe production will provide only one pair a year for each Soviet citizen. Food supplies should be adequate by 1950, at least in starches. But when it comes to such items as meats, fish, sugar, confectionery, wool and cotton fabrics, and footwear, the Plan goes suddenly vague; it merely says that "the marketable stocks . . . shall be greater in 1950 than in 1940." It does promise, though, that "the assortment and finish of fabrics, garments, knitted goods, and footwear must be definitely improved." Even after that 28 per cent increase in retail trade is accomplished, the USSR will have a far smaller flow of commodities than that of any Western country, with the possible exception of Germany and Austria. It will merely raise living standards from the extreme sacrifices of war to a barely tolerable peacetime level.

It is too early to argue that the Kremlin is wrong in imposing another decade or more of hardship and self-denial on the Russian people. If another war does come, these hardships would be a small price to pay for survival. If there is no war, then the heavy industry which is being built at such cost might eventually be turned to producing the good things of life. In that case, the next generation of Russians may enjoy a really substantial rise in living standards.

This policy, however, has two important consequences for the rest of the world.

First of all, it makes impossible the early growth of democracy in the USSR. The Russian people had no real part in making the policy; and neither they nor any other people would tolerate it for a moment if they had a decisive voice in their government. However wise and far sighted it may prove to be, it is a policy which can be maintained only by a dictatorship, armed with an effective political police and propaganda machine.

In the second place, it means that the Soviet people must be kept isolated. If they were allowed to mix with foreigners on any large scale, the contrast between the two standards of living would become impossible to conceal. Once even ten per cent of the Russians learned the truth about the outside world, the government's propaganda would lose its power, and discontent might well get out of hand. Hence only the most trusted Party members can be exposed to the seductive luxuries of the free world, and every American magazine, with its advertisements of electric iceboxes and vacuum cleaners, must be regarded as a subversive influence.

Moreover, if the rest of the world got a good look at Russia, the Communists would lose one of their most useful weapons—the legend that the Soviet Union is The Worker's Paradise. The Kremlin may have the best of reasons for keeping its subjects on short rations for years on end, but the example is not likely to make many converts abroad. Therefore, newspaper correspondents must be kept immured in the Metropole Hotel; their dispatches must be filtered through the tightest kind of censorship; and visitors can be admitted only under the careful shepherding of Intourist.

This means that the wall between Russia and the rest of the world—with all the mistrust and suspicion which it entails—will stand for a long time. It is not merely a Slavic whim, which can be charmed away by lectures about free speech and the need for mutual understanding. It is an essential part of Soviet policy—an indispensable protection for its new series of Five Year Plans. For the next ten years or so, "mutual understanding" between the Russians and other people is one thing which the Kremlin simply cannot afford.

CHAPTER
FOUR

THE SOVIET PRIESTHOOD

IN THEIR EFFORT TO GET READY FOR THE NEXT WAR, the fourteen men who run the Soviet Union have—as we have seen—cut out for themselves two tough jobs. One is domestic, the other foreign. The first is to keep some two hundred million people working at top speed for ten or fifteen years with very little immediate reward. The second is to weld together a solid block of Communist-dominated puppet states, and at the same time to keep the democratic world as weak and divided as possible. The rest of this book is an examination of the tools and methods the Politburo is using to carry out these twin tasks.

Its main instrument for both jobs is, of course, the Communist Party. This is probably the most efficient machine ever devised for the governing of men. It also is a tiny, privileged ruling class, marked off from the great herd it governs as sharply as any ruling class in history. It is a kind of civil service which operates far more effectively than our own. It is a conspiracy, ruthlessly disciplined and masked by secrecy. At the same time, it is a Gallup Poll, recording the whispers of public opinion with four million pairs of ears. It is, as Brooks Atkinson has noted, "a machine for generating power." Above all, it is a blood-brotherhood capable of inspiring the fiercest loyalties. But it is *not* a party.

That word, as the Russians use it, means something utterly different from the normal definition—just as they use the term "democracy" in a sense strange to the rest of the world—and much of our misunderstanding of the Communists grows out of our natural mistake of thinking that their organization bears some resemblance to the GOP or the Democratic Party. It would be much more useful to think of it as a priesthood.

For today the Soviet regime resembles nothing quite so much as it does the government of medieval Spain. The Party, like the ancient religious orders, places its dedicated men in most (though not all) public offices. It alone purveys the True Faith, and its Inquisition, the secret police of the NKVD, mercilessly ferrets out all heretics. It sees its mission as the salvation of all mankind, and any tolerance for the heathen abroad can be nothing less than sin. Its missionaries carry the gospel to benighted lands at the risk of prison, hardship, and sometimes of life itself. And occasionally, like Cortez, they find the sword a great help in making converts.

The rich iconography, always so precious to devout Russians, has not disappeared; it has simply changed a little. Lenin is now the Father, Stalin the Son, and Marx the Holy Ghost, and their pictures are enshrined in almost every home. (Though Marx, appropriately for a Ghost, is not so frequently embodied on the posters and lithographs nowadays. I saw his picture only five times all the

while I was in Russia. The Thirteen Apostles of the Politburo have become much more popular.) Soviet artists today are employed almost exclusively in celebrating these
sacred figures, together with the saints and martyrs of the
Faith; and the conventions of their art are just as rigidly
prescribed as those which the Church once laid down for
the artists of the Middle Ages.

The holy relics are preserved in the Lenin Museum on
the Red Square in Moscow, and replicas have been provided for branch museums in every major city. Before they
view them, the faithful remove their hats, and they stare
with hushed reverence at Lenin's desk, his schoolboy report card, and the wig he wore while hiding from the
Kerensky police. The most sacred relic of all, naturally,
is Lenin's body, displayed in its black marble tomb like the
incorruptible bodies of the saints in the Lavra catacombs.
Every day long lines of worshipers file past the bier, their
faces rapt and grave.

The catechism has been preserved, with minor changes.
In kindergartens I heard the teachers ask: "To whom do
you owe your happy childhood?" And the four-year-olds
lisp: "To Comrade Stalin, hurrah!" (His life-size portrait
was installed on a kind of altar at the front of one class-
room; it was circled by a border of twenty-six colored
electric lights, similar to those used to decorate Christmas
trees.) In the best religious tradition, the Party claims a
monopoly of education, and its rather puritanical moral
code governs the conduct of the people in every detail
from marriage to the reading of books which blaspheme
the revealed doctrine. Moreover, its prelates open nearly

every public meeting with a eulogy of The Leader which is no different, in spirit, from prayer.

Americans think of a political party as a loose sort of organization, open to anyone who bothers to register and exacting no duty more arduous than the occasional marking of a ballot. Becoming a Communist, however, is as difficult as joining the Jesuit order. To anyone who can demonstrate the necessary ability, devotion, and vigor, the door is open, but the screening is so rigorous that only two or three per cent of the Soviet people have been able to gain the coveted membership cards.

When a young Russian aspires to membership in the Party, he renounces the worldly life and dedicates himself to what the Webbs have called "the vocation of leadership." He puts aside all other faiths, including Christianity, and learns to shun such abstruse heresies as "rotten liberalism" and "rightist deviation." After a long apprenticeship in good works and study of the sacred books, his name is put forward by three old members, and if his record, character, and knowledge of the Marxian scriptures can pass the examination of the hierarchy, he finally is sworn into the order.

From that day forward, his life belongs to the Kremlin. He may be ordered, without notice, to report for duty in Vienna or the Arctic Circle, to fight an epidemic in Kazakstan, instruct a band of Manchurian guerrillas, or filch atomic secrets in Ottawa. He can make no moral judgments of his own, because all righteousness now lies in one thing: unquestioning obedience to the organization. He has no private life, for his behavior, papers, and thoughts are under constant scrutiny; he feels the watchful presence of the NKVD far more oppressively than does the ordinary Soviet citizen. He may be unfrocked for drunkenness, sexual scandal, laziness, or the slightest wavering from the Party line. If his indiscretion is serious enough, he may be condemned to a labor camp or shot out of hand, as thousands of Communists were during the bloody months of 1937. For minor transgressions, however, a few months' penance in a lonely or unpleasant assignment usually is the only punishment. On holy days, such as May Day and the November 7 anniversary of the revolution, the pious Communist makes his pilgrimage to the Red Square or at least to the celebration at the local shrine. He even keeps his chin clean-shaven, as the monks shaved their crowns; a beardless face is one of the caste marks which few modern Communists aside from Lenin and the late, revered Papa Kalinin have ever cared to ignore.

Such a tightly-disciplined organization obviously has elements of great strength. It can move as swiftly and secretly as a well-trained army, without wasting time in debate or bogging down in compromise. It attracts the ablest and most ambitious men, because it is the only ladder to power and to all the dignities and perquisites that go with it. Moreover, the Party's internal administration—directed by Stalin himself and by his bright, tough young man, Georgi Malenkov—so far has been extraordinarily competent. Men of capacity have risen swiftly to responsible jobs, and the deadwood has been pruned away without compassion.

Inevitably the Party also attracts some opportunists and sly scoundrels, as the 1946 purge of grafting factory managers revealed; but these, I believe, are rather rare exceptions. During the course of my work in the Soviet Union I found no trace of the pervading corruption, the sadism and moral deformity which were so evident among the ruling elite of Nazi Germany. Most of the Party members with whom I worked impressed me as sincere and honest men—idealists, many of them, who are convinced that they are serving a sacred cause.

Such a man was Vassily Vladimirovich Khomyak (pronounced hom-yahk), my closest acquaintance among the Ukrainians. He was in charge of the special agency set up by the Ukrainian government to handle the distribution of UNRRA supplies, and my duties threw me with him nearly every day and often far into the night. I have never known a more conscientious public servant, or a pleasanter drinking companion.

Vassily was a wiry little man with a tired, wizened face and instinctively gentle manners. His expression ordinarily was one of harassed patience; I never once saw him lose his temper, in spite of maddening and innumerable provocations. When they became unendurable, he would merely sigh, run his fingers through his rumpled tussock of graying hair, and grit his stainless-steel teeth. (That's the usual material for bridgework in the USSR because of the shortage of dental porcelain. About half of Vassily's bicuspids and incisors had been replaced with nice, shiny dentures.) Since he was a relatively high-level bureaucrat, reporting directly to the Council of Ministers, Khomyak could afford to dress nattily. Ordinarily he wore a sober gray or tan suit, gray kidskin oxfords, and a bright blue rayon polo shirt; his hat was blue velour, with a lush nap.

On special occasions, however, he wore the blue-and-khaki dress uniform and the five medals—each as big as a fried egg—which he had earned as a colonel of Partisans fighting behind the German lines. His band of some eighteen hundred men had led a life of grinding hardship, sleeping in the snow, going hungry for days on end, marching to the very edge of exhaustion to massacre some unsuspecting Reichswehr outpost and then to escape the pursuing column. (Once Vassily timed a raid to catch a Nazi major on the day of his marriage to a renegade Ukrainian girl. He thought it a great joke that his tommy-gunners had mowed down the major, bride, and wedding guests while the ceremony was in full swing.) Four years of such strain had left Khomyak prematurely aged and broken in health. He suffered almost continual pain from asthma and a tired heart, and he made no secret of his belief that his time was fast running out.

Yet he worked man-killing hours. Vassily reached his office at about ten in the morning, left around five for lunch and a few minutes' rest, and then came back to his desk to stay until long after midnight. Such hours are part of the Bolshevik tradition; ever since Lenin, the Communist leaders have made a habit of working far into the night, and pouches under the eyes have become almost a badge of Party membership.

In Vassily's case, there were additional reasons. He had a huge and intricate task, a new and not yet entirely dependable staff, and—perhaps worst of all—a group of American investigators who constantly needled him for detailed reports on what was happening to UNRRA's supplies and to the Ukraine's home-grown food. Frequently he himself handled quite minor chores, such as making plane reservations for us or digging up rationing statistics, apparently because there was no one to whom he could delegate such details with confidence that they would be done on schedule.

For his agency suffered from a weakness which seems to afflict almost every administrative organization in Russia—a desperate shortage of trained personnel on the lower levels. Vassily's two or three top assistants were fairly competent operators, but below them he had a straggling collection of clerks and bookkeepers who were, in many cases, only a few years away from peasantry.

This particular weakness is not the fault of any individual, or the Party, or even of the Soviet economic system. It is simply one of the unavoidable difficulties of a nation which is trying within a single generation to change itself from a drove of sluggish, ignorant peasants into a modern industrial state. Much the same thing happened in England during the early stages of its Industrial Revolution, although there the transformation was slower and the thick-fingered yeomanry could be housebroken at a more leisurely pace.

(In many other aspects of Russian life, it seems to me, things which are commonly praised or blamed as the fruits of Communism are, in fact, nothing of the kind. They are merely the fruits of a belated Industrial Revolution. It is largely coincidence that in Russia this revolution in technology took place at the same time as a revolution in politics. But it is only human nature that the Communists should claim credit for the more spectacular results—the huge increase in farm machinery, for example, and the rapid growth of military strength. After all, the nineteenth-century British Liberals garnered credit for similar blessings of the machine, which happened to coincide with the ascendancy of their pet theory of capitalism. And it is also natural that the enemies of Communism should blame it for the dreary by-products of industrialization—the overcrowded cities, the factory worker's loss of personal independence, the countless wrenching social adjustments —just as Karl Marx once blamed these same evils on "capitalism.")

Because the Germans had destroyed many of Kiev's public buildings, Khomyak had housed his eighty-odd employees in a shabby, hastily-repaired three-story apartment on Pushkin Street. It smelled of damp plaster, and until late spring it was so cold that every breath showed as a frosty plume. The girls wore their overcoats all day, and their stiff, chilblained fingers didn't make for speedy typing. Khomyak's own office on the top floor was as cold and sparely furnished as the rest. It contained only his wooden desk, a long conference table covered with blue cloth, a battered brown safe with an eight-inch key, two water carafes, and a dozen straight-backed chairs. The walls, however, had been freshly painted with elaborate floral designs stenciled to simulate wallpaper, and they were hung with the usual oversized portraits of Stalin, Molotov, Khrushchev, and Shevchenko, the local Bobby Burns. The only personal touch in the room was Vassily's pencil holder, a little plaster mug decorated with a carving of a hound dog with a rabbit in its mouth.

The staff worked at a relaxed and desultory pace, interrupted by frequent tea drinking and long, rambling conversations. (The methodical organization of his own time is a knack which the average Russian has not yet acquired.) It was also handicapped by a shortage of all kinds of office equipment. The whole agency had only five typewriters, for example—valued at fifteen hundred dollars each—and the secretaries had never seen a typewriter eraser. When we loaned them a few, together with such other unheard-of gadgets as a stapling machine and a roll of Scotch tape, they were as pleased as children with a new toy. Telephones, too, were both scarce and temperamental. No Soviet executive tries to transact much business by phone, aside from the making of appointments, and even that is likely to fray his vocal chords.

It was a little unexpected, therefore, to find that the organization somehow got its work done with considerable efficiency. Every month it routed some twenty-five thousand tons of relief supplies from the Odessa wharves to hundreds of cities and villages—and, on the whole, the right things got to the right places on time. Moreover, losses from pilferage and careless handling were notably small, and swiftly punished. If there was any blackmarketing or graft in UNRRA goods, we were never able to discover it.

From our earliest dealings with the Ukrainian government, it was apparent that its inner wheels moved much like those of any other bureaucracy—not according to the formal organization chart, that is, but along a delicate network of personal relationships.

In theory, Khomyak got his orders from Nikita Khrushchev, governor of the republic, and his entire Council of Ministers. (These cabinet officers originally were called People's Commissars—a term gleefully adopted by Lenin, because "it smells terribly of revolution." The more respectable title of "minister" was adopted this spring—presumably because years of anti-Soviet propaganda have given "commissar" such a hair-raising connotation. A Goebbels could give an audience the shivers when he asked: "How would you like to have your daughter raped by a drunken commissar?" But substitute the word "minister" and the question sounds downright ridiculous.) In practice, however, Khomyak preferred to take his troubles to his guardian angel among the heavy brass—a handsome young man named I. S. Senin, vice-chairman of the Council and one of Boss Khrushchev's fair-haired boys.

Senin, who was built like a football player and might easily be mistaken for a junior vice-president of the National City Bank, had studied chemical engineering at Columbia in 1931 and he still enjoyed talking English. He wore impeccably-cut blue pin-stripe suits—the best I saw in all Russia—smoked Lucky Strikes (imported by diplomatic courier), and talked with crisp, good-humored confidence. Since his job is the running of all industry in the Ukraine, it was hardly surprising that he suffered from stomach ulcers, the occupational disease of top government executives in all countries. When he was away for treatment at a sanatorium in the Caucasus mountains, Khomyak had a good deal of difficulty in getting quick decisions out of the rest of the Council—"they just shove my memos under their desk blotters"—but when Senin got back to town, the memos were pulled out again and things began to happen fast.

From their subordinates the ministers got a degree of deference which would have embarrassed most American bureaucrats. When Khomyak went with us to a conference with Senin or The Boss, for example, he always stopped in the anteroom to comb his hair, straighten his tie, and take a couple of quick licks at his shoes with the brush which was kept on a little shoeshine stand provided for the convenience of visitors. Once inside the conference room, he shrank into the least conspicuous chair, listened with alert nervousness, and spoke only when someone asked him a question.

A visit to one of the ministers, incidentally, was a matter of considerable ceremony. As our car pulled up before the eleven-story building which houses the Council, we were always met by a uniformed NKVD officer, who escorted us past the heavily armed sentries at the entrance and the guards, with rifle and bayonet, stationed at intervals in the corridors. Each door swung open before us, and closed silently as soon as we had passed through. (I never found out how that trick was worked; spooks, maybe.) The inner office of every big-shot had two doors with a two-foot air space between them. As a further discouragement to eaves-droppers, these doors were heavily padded with imitation leather, and little plates covered the keyholes.

Within the Council there seemed to be a healthy amount of bureaucratic rivalry over such questions as the splitting up of a 127-ton shipment of UNRRA sole leather. The Minister of Trade wanted most of it for shoes, the Minister of Health insisted on at least forty-five tons for the manu-facture of artificial limbs, while another of their colleagues schemed to get all he could for industrial belting. A similar argument dragged on for weeks over whether UNRRA vitamins should be classed as a medicine, charged against the Health Ministry's allocation, or a food which would be chargeable to the Ministry of Trade.

This kind of politicking went on all the way down the line. The mayor of Poltava, for instance, took off a whole day to show us the urgent needs of his ruined city. When he finally put us on the train at two o'clock one morning, well-banqueted and primed with vodka, he remarked that he had complete confidence in the Council's fairness in distributing relief supplies among the many war-ravaged cities. But when we got back to Kiev, would we please put in a good word with The Boss about the altogether unique case of Poltava?

In the end, all such questions were refereed by Khrush-chev, one of the fourteen most powerful men in Russia by virtue of his seat on the Communist Party Politburo. At fifty-two he looks at least a decade older—rather like a beardless, blue-eyed Santa Claus on the morning after a hard Christmas—because, his friends say, he almost worked himself to death during the war. The son of a Kursk miner, he labored in the mines himself until he joined the Party in 1918. From then on he rose fast, handling one tough job after another with a marked flair for organization. During the Great Purge, Stalin sent him in to boss the stiff-necked Ukrainians, whose native political leaders had got them-selves liquidated for treason. Now, although they never forget that he is an outsider, many Ukrainians speak of him with what seems to be genuine affection and respect.

The day-to-day performance of the men who run the Ukraine seemed to me about as good as any I've ever seen in the last fifteen years, during which my chief business has been reporting on the behavior of bureaucrats. They would measure up pretty well, for example, beside such smooth-running outfits as the United States Forest Service or the Republican machine in Westchester County. Nearly all of them have that quiet pride in their jobs which is one of the universal earmarks of a competent organiza-tion. (The typical Ukrainian mayor radiates an enthusiasm for his city which would shame a California Chamber of Commerce secretary; I kept feeling that each of them was about to sell me a lot.) Allowing for the many handicaps under which it operates, the Ukrainian government must,

I think, be credited with reasonable honesty, vigor, and effectiveness.

The men who run it also argue, with all sincerity, that it is a democratic government. To them, democracy means government *for* the people, and they unquestionably are working for what they believe to be the long-run good of all Soviet citizens. Or, anyhow, what the Politburo has decided is good for them.

There is no pretense, of course, of government *by* the people, nor any real understanding of what it means. The Communist regards "the nonparty masses" as a herd of lazy, slow-witted, bearlike creatures, benumbed by centuries of serfdom, who have to be coaxed and chivvied along the road to The Perfect Society by the Party shepherds. The common man cannot be trusted to decide what is good for him, because he would almost surely want nothing more than a full belly, warm clothes, and a long nap on top of the brick stove. Certainly he is not farsighted enough to choose the bone-cracking labor and the endless self-denial which are demanded by the new series of Five Year Plans.

Public policy, therefore, must be left in the hands of the elite, who are specially trained to deal with such matters. The people may be permitted to vote, because voting is one of the traditional trimmings of "democracy." But there is no need, so far as the Communist can see, to confuse them by putting more than one name on the ballot. Indeed, the very idea of admitting a second party to an election would strike him as wicked. After all, he knows that the Communist Party is infallibly right, by what amounts to divine revelation. All other parties, therefore, must be wrong, and nothing but evil could come of permitting them to spread their disturbing heresies.

These views seem to have the approval—or at least the acquiescence—of the great majority of Russians. They have never had a taste of democratic self-government in all their history. They don't know what it is, and, so far as I could tell, they don't especially want it. In all their experience, ruling has been the business of professional rulers, whether khan, czar, or commissar. For centuries these rulers were harsh, arbitrary, and incompetent. Now they are harsh, a little less arbitrary, and far more competent. Nearly everybody is grateful for the obvious improvement.

Moreover, the present government is closer to the people than any they have ever known. Each local Communist leader keeps in touch with his flock like a parish priest. If he hopes for a brilliant future, he also looks after them with the zeal of a Tammany district leader. He attends their weddings and village dances—perhaps obliging with a few well-chosen words about The Leader—and he's the man to see if somebody needs an extra load of firewood or a travel permit to visit Aunt Tanya in Odessa.

More important still, he listens sympathetically to their complaints—or, at any rate, to any complaints about the way in which The Plan is being carried out. (Nobody is fool enough to complain about The Plan itself.) If the beef sounds reasonable, he tries to fix things up, carrying the fight if necessary clear up to the Party Central Committee in Kiev. When such criticisms become loud and numerous enough, there may be some change in local administrators or in the application of policy, for the Party has a strong sense of what the traffic will bear.

One result of all this is that the ward heelers of Dnepropetrovsk and Darnitsa have come to look and behave very much like the ward heelers in Pittsburgh or Memphis —hearty extroverts with the ever-ready smile, the big hello, the manly handshake, the sure-fire memory for first names. Once I visited a kindergarten in Kharkov with a local politician named Peter Petrovich Sachko. He patted all the kids on the head and ended up with a little speech in which he mentioned his own name, with some emphasis, ten times in as many minutes. You would have thought that the next election was heavy on his mind; and perhaps it was. True enough, his constituents would have to vote for the lone candidate whom the Party put on the ballot; but the Party does not often renominate officials who prove unpopular.

Public disgruntlement is, in fact, sometimes deliberately channeled against some luckless functionary, when it is necessary to deflect criticism from the Party. Actually, of course, the Party and the government are as inseparable as the two sides of a ruble note, but the press often makes a sharp distinction between them. Whatever goes wrong is blamed on "the bureaucrats" and "office rats"; but when there is praise to be ladled out, it goes to the Party dignitaries who led the enterprise to its glorious conclusion.

Thus, the Ukrainian *Pravda* turned loose a shattering

blast, in its issue of April 17, 1946, against certain bureau-crats of Zaporozhe under the headline "Why Did Buttons and Steel Knives Become a Problem?"

The article deplored "the inability of buying anywhere in the city a button, a table knife, a fork, shoe polish, and other 'trifles' needed daily," and added: "The Regional Office of Local Industry—of which Comrade Bronnikov is the chief—was supposed to give the market seventeen kinds of manufactured goods last year, among them buttons, spoons, and knives. But it issued only six, and among them one does not find goods of which there is a great shortage in the region. . . .

"The Regional Co-operative—Chairman, Comrade Marinchenko—had a quota of fifteen hundred pails, but manufactured only two; instead of one thousand cane chairs, only eighty-four. Many leaders of local industry ignore the plans . . . with impunity. All this occurs only because of the fact that Zaporozhe when making its plans does not take care of the main condition necessary for their execution, i.e. daily control, and they are unable to develop initiative and ingenuity."

Nowhere in this item—which is a fairly typical example of the famed "socialist self-criticism"—was there any mention of the Communist Party. Nor was there any hint that the great bulk of Zaporozhe's resources was being poured at that moment into the reconstruction of the city's great steel mill, in accordance with the Five Year Plan, instead of into the making of those urgently-needed consumers' goods.

Incidentally, nobody could tell me what happened to

Comrades Bronnikov and Marinchenko, but it probably is a safe bet that they've taken up some other line of work.

The very characteristics which give the Soviet political system much of its strength—stern discipline and tight central control—also are responsible for certain critical weaknesses.

The most obvious of these is the reluctance of nearly all minor bureaucrats to shoulder responsibility. The penalties for a mistake are so drastic that no sensible man is eager to make an important decision on his own. If he guesses wrong—no matter how honestly—his mistake may not be accepted as mere bad judgment. Quite possibly he may face criminal charges of sabotage and treason, followed by the grim punishments reserved for "enemies of the people."

Consequently, he is careful to get plenty of counter-signatures on every document, to clear every step with his superiors and the local Party authorities, and to build a shield of detailed paper records. The result is endless conferences, red tape, and delay. My first contact with Russian officialdom was in Berlin, where a thoroughly obliging Soviet trade representative named Lebensohn pleaded with his colleagues by phone for nearly two hours to get a document authorizing our party to board a plane for Moscow. In the end he got it only by agreeing to add his own signature—that is, by putting his neck on the line, too. True enough, the Soviet red tape was no worse than that of the American army in Berlin; but in the USSR nearly every transaction has to be handled "through channels," with all the frustrations which, in most other countries, are limited to the military establishments.

Even if a Russian official were foolhardy enough to try to act on his own in the interests of getting the job done fast, he would never be permitted to exercise full responsibility. For in every organization authority is split three ways—among the nominal management, the Party, and the NKVD. A hospital director, for example, told me that he dared not make any important move without consulting one of his subordinates, who happened to be the secretary of the hospital's Party cell. A similar Communist organization exists among the employees of every factory, bureau, and collective farm, and one of its main functions is to spot any sign of bungling or "sabotage" by the manager. Moreover, both the management and the members of the Party cell work under the suspicious eye of the NKVD, which has its secret agents planted within every organization of consequence. Those police spies have keys to all safes and filing cabinets, and no visitor or phone call is likely to escape their attention.

The same system of multiple watchdogs apparently operates in Soviet establishments abroad. The report of the Canadian Royal Commission investigating Russian espionage, for example, noted that Comrade Goussarov, a second secretary in the Ottawa embassy, wielded authority "on the level of the ambassador," for Goussarov was organizer of the Party's central committee within the embassy. Another second secretary, Comrade Pavlov, ran the NKVD, and his spies sometimes tripped over another espionage network directed by Colonel Zabotin, the military attaché. Both operated quite independently of the ambassador, who was not even permitted to read their cables or enter their offices.

In Washington the Party's head man is generally believed to be an obscure official of the Soviet Purchasing Commission named Serov. Victor Kravchenko, a backsliding Communist who ran away from that Commission, in his recent book described Serov as "the most potent agent of the Soviet state in America," whose "word was law for everyone, from the most menial Soviet employee to the most important. . . ."

The basic reason for all this divided responsibility and mistrust is, of course, that pervading fear—the dominant characteristic of the Soviet hierarchy—which was discussed in an earlier chapter. So long as the men in the Kremlin feel threatened by crowding dangers, both within their borders and from abroad, they cannot bring themselves to place full trust in any subordinate.

Another reason lies in the history of the Party. It was founded as an underground conspiracy, fighting for its life against the spies and hangmen of the czarist police. It could survive only by developing its own system of counterespionage and secrecy, backed by merciless punishments. As a result, the organization grew into a mold which it could never break, even after it had swept into power. Men who have spent their youth as conspirators—listening constantly for a step on the stairs, never for a moment quite free of anxiety—are seldom able to shake off the old habits entirely. Even today, therefore, and even within Russia itself, the Party still operates on a semi-conspiratorial basis. Nobody talks freely about its affairs, and its inner workings are never mentioned in the press. The members themselves rarely know what goes on outside their immediate circle, and they are held as strictly accountable for every word and action as if they were still part of an underground.

This harsh, conspiratorial tradition has some amusing results. One of them is eager-beaverism, a disease especially prevalent among Soviet representatives abroad. These sorely tried patriots know that they are under a doubly suspicious surveillance all the while they are exposed to the temptations of the capitalist world. They also know that they have to get results, or else. Consequently, when a Russian is sent on a foreign mission he often makes almost hysterical efforts to prove his loyalty and build a shining record. In Washington, for example, the Soviet Purchasing Commission quite evidently had orders to get all the UNRRA supplies it could and to pile them on shipboard fast—and the Kremlin wasn't interested in excuses about food shortages or the needs of other countries.

The Russian representatives thereupon made themselves the world's champion needlers. They followed every requisition, minute by minute, on its tortuous course through the bureaucratic labyrinth, prodding at every step. Clouds of excited, arm-waving Slavs besieged the offices of UNRRA and the Treasury and Agriculture Department procurement agencies, demanding to know why that tractor contract hadn't been filled or protesting a ten-minute delay in the signing of a purchase order for two tons of clover seed.

The result, of course, was precisely the opposite of what was intended. American officials came to dread the sound of a Russian voice, and out of sheer harassment they sometimes got stubborn and refused to be hustled. In the end their blowtorch tactics probably did the Soviet agents a good deal more harm than good.

The same kind of eager-beaverism sometimes backfires on the Russian government at home. The widespread falsification of production figures which was uncovered during the purge of industrial officials this summer was partly caused, no doubt, by an ordinary human hankering for juicier bonuses. But a more important reason, I suspect, was the unrelenting pressure on every factory manager to hang up bigger and bigger output records. When he can't meet the schedule, because of shortages of material, skilled labor, or equipment, the plant executive is subject to almost overwhelming temptation to cook his figures. He risks trouble, naturally, if the forgery is discovered; but he is *sure* of trouble if his production records fail to show "fulfillment of the plan."

The secrecy which goes along with the Communists' conspiratorial habits also has some unfortunate by-products. One of them is a surprising ignorance of what, in any other country, would be public affairs. Khomyak, for example, was supposedly the best-informed man in the Ukraine about UNRRA activities. Yet he was astonished to learn—from Americans—that several Soviet citizens were employed by UNRRA both in its Washington and London headquarters and in responsible field positions. Moreover, he had only the vaguest notions about the work of the Soviet Purchasing Commission or the movements of Russian ships carrying UNRRA goods.

Such unfamiliarity with their own government, plus an all but complete ignorance of the outside world, may account for much of the Soviet Union's difficulty in recruiting competent men for foreign service from the lower ranks of its bureaucracy. I had to deal with one official— a specialist in foreign trade—who was firmly convinced that Philadelphia was on the west coast of America and who had made up his shipping schedules accordingly.

But these are minor flaws in comparison with the two really serious weaknesses of the Soviet political machine. One of them is an overcentralization of decisions; the other is a blind inflexibility in official thinking.

During the war all of us heard a lot of talk about the enviable ability of the dictatorships to make decisions rapidly. This is undoubtedly true of the big decisions—those which may switch a whole nation on the track from peace to war. It can be argued, however, that these are the very decisions which ought *not* to be made quickly, which should be reached only after long and searching public debate. For if one of them turns out wrong, the results— as Hitler and Mussolini learned—may be fatal, and not for the dictator alone.

It is equally true, though less generally recognized, that

a highly centralized government is utterly incapable of making little decisions promptly. The reluctance of small-fry bureaucrats to take on responsibility, which we have already noted, means that thousands of petty, day-to-day problems—whether to pave a twenty-mile stretch of road or when to hire an extra clerk—pile up on the desks of Higher Authority. There it is physically impossible to handle them with dispatch—as anyone who ever had to deal with wartime Washington well knows.

Yet if this kind of decision is not made swiftly and on the spot, the whole machinery of government clogs up. When a Soviet purchasing agent found, for instance, that one brand of machine tool was not immediately available in America, he could not switch his contract to another of almost identical make; for weeks he had to await authority from Moscow, while some Russian factory stood idle. A Soviet consul cannot even grant a visa without cabling for permission; and when I was ready to leave Moscow it took me three days to get an exit permit, even with the help of several rank-laden officials. The cumulative effect of such trifling but innumerable stoppages is a dragging tempo, a hidden waste of manpower, which may turn out to be a permanent handicap in the Soviet Union's race to overtake the western nations.

For this is not the sort of trouble which can be cured by efficiency experts or shrewder management. It is inherent, I believe, in the very nature of large, centralized organizations. It can be discerned, on a smaller scale, in some of our mammoth corporations, where it provides one of the strongest arguments for the trust busters. Our

American habit of dispersing both economic and political decisions among thousands of independent units—state legislatures, trade unions, school districts, small businesses, TVA, farm co-operatives, port authorities, public power districts, and countless others—sometimes looks hopelessly disorderly. But it may conceal a peculiar strength which we have not yet fully appreciated.

A still more fundamental handicap for the Russians is the mental rigidity which seems to afflict nearly everyone who has been schooled in Marxist doctrine. The thoroughly trained Communist tends to think in formulas, which he has been assured will provide the infallible answer to every question. If a fact doesn't quite fit, he would never dream of revising the formula, for that would be heresy; he simply rejects the fact.

A classic example is the Communist policy for the American Negro. Stalin, who earned his early reputation as Lenin's expert on racial problems, had devised a scheme which worked pretty well in Russia. It called for an "autonomous" republic for each separate nationality, thus permitting the Uzbeks, Tatars, Kazaks, and other peoples of the USSR to preserve some remnants of their individual cultures. Inevitably the Communists in this country adopted the same formula, letter for letter, as their solution for America's racial problem. They proposed to carve an autonomous Negro republic out of the heart of the Southern states.

Unfortunately for them, this simple recipe did not take into account two glaring facts: (1) many Negroes didn't want to stay in the South; (2) almost none of them wanted a Jim Crow republic, which might well freeze forever the discrimination that is their real grievance. As a result, the Negroes—who might otherwise have been the Party's easiest converts—have never flocked in any paying number to buy its patent medicine. To this day, however, the Communists have not changed their formula. They merely deplore the stubborn refusal of the Negroes to swallow Old Doctor Stalin's Wonderful Remedy. (Some of the Central Asiatic tribesmen gagged a little, too, in the beginning, but the Red Army finally poured it down their throats.)

Because they are drilled to think in such stereotyped patterns—all dictated by a few men who are profoundly ignorant of the outside world—the Communists may run into increasing difficulties as they attempt to expand their operations beyond the Russian borders. The effective opposition of Europe's Catholic parties has been demonstrated in every recent election, but in addition, the going may prove unexpectedly tough in the Protestant countries, such as England and the United States.

For the appeal of Communism, it seems to me, is essentially religious. It purports to offer not merely a political program but a road to salvation for all the world. Although its ritual is couched in materialistic terms, it demands a mystic devotion surpassing all other loyalties. Moreover—and this is the central point—it preaches an authoritarian theology. The Kremlin, a sort of Red Vatican, is the sole fountainhead of the faith, claiming supreme authority on all questions of doctrine.

This kind of theology may not go down very easily among peoples who have been accustomed for centuries to interpreting religious dogma for themselves. The Protestant tradition still has a good deal of strength, even among many Americans who are no longer churchgoers; at least they are slow to acknowledge that any authority can be superior to their own consciences. Moreover, they have an ingrained habit of tolerance for many sects, a belief that righteousness lies in a man's personal behavior rather than in meek obedience to a hierarchy, and a feeling that it is old fashioned and somehow barbarous to burn noncomformists at the stake. Such people, then, will not readily accept the Communists' violent suppression of heretics, nor the doctrine that every action—including lying, treason, and murder—is morally correct if performed in the service of The Cause.

It would be foolish not to recognize that the Communists have hit upon a formidable system of organization, which has worked with considerable effectiveness in Russia. But it would be equally naïve to assume that the same kind of political priesthood can operate successfully in the very different context of the western world.

CHAPTER FIVE

THE CLASSLESS SOCIETY, KIND OF

A FAVORITE STORY AMONG THE AMERICANS IN Moscow is about the romance of a soldier who worked in the embassy. He met a curvesome and amiable chorus girl from the Bolshoi Theater, and tender passion blossomed with gratifying promptness. Eventually, however, they had a lovers' spat, and the soldier lost his temper. After bitter words on both sides, he finally blurted:

"Why, you're nothing but a first-class whore!"

"You can't talk that way to me," she answered, as the tears started down her cheeks. "In the Soviet Union there are no classes!"

She was simply repeating an article of faith which is close to the heart of every good Soviet citizen. The great pride of the Communists is their success in establishing what they call "the first classless society," and never for a moment do they let you forget it. Even the railroads shun the evil word; tickets are sold for first, second, and third "categories" of accommodations. On the lines running through the Ukraine, First Category passengers ride either two or four to a compartment and their berths are covered with green cushions. Second Category or "hard" compartments have nine uncushioned wooden bunks, hung three deep on three of the four walls. Third Category accommodations are similar, except that bunks cannot be reserved. In all categories it is customary for men and women to share the same compartments and washrooms. (In addition, there are three other modes of rail travel: the pre-1918 *wagon-lits* "luxury" cars sometimes provided for foreigners and very important bureaucrats; space on the corridor floors, couplings, and car roofs for people who can't afford a seat; and the NKVD prison cars, heavily barred and guarded, for political offenders and other criminals.)

When a Communist says that there are no classes in Russia, he means it in all sincerity, but, as so often happens, he is using a word in a sense quite different from its meaning in the outside world. He does *not* mean that there is equality in either rank or wealth among all citizens—for Lenin explicitly stated that such equality is not one of the goals of Communism. All he means is that no private individual controls land, machinery, or other "instruments of production" which might enable him to "exploit" people who do not own such property. Even by this definition there is some question—as we shall note a little later— about how classless Russian society actually is.

When an American speaks of classes he usually is thinking of differences in living standards, education, and social standing. Class distinctions in this sense do exist in the USSR, sometimes to even greater degree than in the

United States. (No Russian ever denies this fact, although American Communists occasionally do.) Moreover, class privileges are created by the government itself, frankly and deliberately, as one of the main tools for enforcing its policies. They run through every aspect of Soviet life, from the distribution of power down to the handing out of theater tickets. There is even some evidence that they may become hereditary, as the privileges of the ruling class tend to do in every form of society.

There is a venerable Russian legend about the master who got an astonishing amount of work out of his serfs by using two means of persuasion—a cookie and a whip. The moral has not been forgotten. Today the Soviet rulers are using the same carefully-balanced combination of rewards and punishments to squeeze the greatest possible effort out of their weary subjects. It is an effective method —probably the only one, in fact, which could ever succeed in creating a giant war industry within the brief period set by the Five Year Plans. This chapter and the next are concerned with the way in which the Soviet regime doles out its cookies. Later we shall see how it uses the whip.

The rewards in Russia, naturally enough, go to those who prove especially useful to the state. Distribution is in the hands of the party bosses, who sometimes take a liberal view of their own deserts—just as American corporation executives now and then encourage themselves with over-generous bonuses. Aside from this normal human failing, however, the prizes seem to be parceled out with a reasonably fair regard for the Soviet yardsticks of merit. These are unhesitating obedience, ability, and hard work, in that order.

Of all the many kinds of rewards, money is perhaps the least important. There are, of course, wide differences in income. A lieutenant in the Red Army, for example, gets one hundred times as much as a private, while in the American army the difference in pay between the same ranks is only about three to one. Factory managers, government officials, and skilled workers enjoy handsome salaries, plus bonuses and sometimes expense accounts. Recently priests of the Russian Orthodox Church also have climbed into the upper-income brackets, for reasons noted in the next chapter. There are even a few ruble millionaires, mostly among the more popular authors, who get huge royalties from the sale of their books. It is probably the only country in the world where a mine-run poet can earn ten thousand dollars a year. (Exceptionally high pay has proved necessary to keep writers producing in the Soviet Union, since they are denied that free use of the intellect which normally is the main incentive of the artist. Even so, the results often are far from satisfactory. The literary magazine *Leningrad* had to be closed down in August 1946 because it had published "ideologically alien" stories and poems, which—as *Pravda* put it—ignored "the vital foundation of the Soviet system, its political policy." At about the same time many fiction writers and playwrights got a tongue-lashing in the Party press because they seemed to pay more attention to "art for art's sake" than to "the principles of Bolshevik partisanship in art.")

A big income is less attractive than it would be elsewhere, however, because there is so little to buy with it. A ruble, in fact, is simply a piece of paper which will buy something when accompanied by enough other documents; by itself it is often useless. Consequently, the really enticing prizes are such things as special ration privileges, special living quarters, automobiles, fancy offices, and positions of authority.

And, of course, medals. Nearly everybody in the USSR has at least one medal, and many people have six or seven. They wear them, too—not just the ribbons but the medals themselves, both on uniforms and civilian clothes. I met one eight-year-old boy who had two decorations pinned on his well-patched shirt, one for helping the Partisans, the other for a shrapnel wound which had gouged out a three-inch strip of his scalp. A waiter in our Kiev hotel had a nice little red-and-white enamel number for faithful service in a war-factory dining room. Once I sat across a banquet table from a general whose front was covered from belt to collarbone with bejeweled medals as big as sunflowers. (The highest order is the plainest—a chaste gold star on a red ribbon, given to Heroes of the Soviet Union. It is worn on the left breast above all others. Stalin usually appears with this medal alone.)

The really handsome emoluments fall almost entirely to the four privileged classes: (1) the upper-crust bureaucrats, (2) army officers, (3) technicians—engineers, scientists, doctors, authors—and (4) the so-called Stakhanovites, or workers who make abnormally high production records.

The big men in the Party, who hold the key jobs

throughout the bureaucracy, live very well indeed. The office from which Khrushchev runs the Ukraine, for example, is about twice the size of the President's White House study, and its furnishings are far more luxurious. Two yellow marble pillars divide the room in halves, one of which is dominated by The Boss's big carved desk and the other by a conference table as large as the dance floor in a small night club. Thick-piled oriental rugs cover the floor. The walls are paneled in some dark, polished wood which I could not identify—perhaps Circassian walnut—and they are hung with the inevitable portraits of Stalin and Lenin. These are oil paintings, however, instead of the usual lithographs, and they are flanked by similar pictures of three military heroes, Suvorov, Kutuzov, and Khmelnitsky. The nearest equivalent in this country would be the board room of a major corporation, or the majestic suite built by Herbert Hoover for the secretaries of the Commerce Department. Khrushchev's subordinates on the Ukraine Council of Ministers have offices which are less elaborate but still a cut above the quarters assigned to most American bureaucrats of equivalent rank.

The Boss, moreover, enjoys a home in Kiev that would do credit to a Long Island millionaire; he also is said to have an apartment in the Kremlin, a country place thirty miles outside of Moscow, and a villa in the Caucasus for vacations. For entertaining visiting firemen he has a separate guesthouse of truly oriental splendor at 17 Levamovski Street in the most fashionable section of Kiev. It had been badly damaged by the Germans, and when I saw it the repairs had just been completed. Some of the furnishings had not yet been installed, but the frescoed ceilings, satin wall coverings, and intricately carved woodwork were all in place. So was a white-lacquered grand piano, encrusted with gold leaf, and a massive banquet table which comfortably seated fifty guests. The one dinner I attended there might have come straight out of *The Arabian Nights*. It lasted from eight in the evening until nearly 2 A.M., with liveried waiters—one to each place—marching in with what seemed like an endless procession of courses, ranging from caviar (four varieties) through soup, fish, game, meat, and salad to a dazzling array of sweets and fruit. The innumerable toasts were drunk in vodka, cognac, champagne, and assorted Russian wines. I got home sober only through the kindly offices of a Ukrainian interpreter, who helped keep my vodka glass surreptitiously filled with mineral water after the first toast.

(It was at this banquet, incidentally, that a leading member of the Ukrainian government asked me whether "all progressive Americans live in the Southern states." Senator Pepper came from the South, didn't he? While the North kept electing that dangerous reactionary, Senator Vandenberg?)

Such gaudy feasts do not, however, mean that the top Communists habitually wallow in gluttonous luxury while their people go hungry—although a few American visitors have jumped to that conclusion. They do enjoy a party, and when they get a chance they eat and drink with gusto. But normally they get such a chance only when some traveling official provides an excuse for enter-

tainment. Then they go in for lavish feeding primarily because the Asiatic tradition of hospitality demands it. Food
has a symbolic importance, just as it does in India and
China, which for centuries have never felt quite safe from
starvation. In addition, the Soviets, like the czars, regard a
big banquet as a minor but useful political instrument; it
is intended to impress foreigners with the wealth and splendor of the regime.

The workaday meals of Russia's ruling class are far less
bacchanalian—nobody could get drunk every night and
still turn out the amount of work expected of a Communist—but they are a good deal better than the fare of
common citizens. For high officials, army officers, scientists, teachers, and certain other privileged groups there
are special ration stores which the ordinary Russian is not
even permitted to enter. Here they find a considerably
greater variety of goods, usually of better quality, than
they would in the shops catering to the masses. A colonel,
for example, may be entitled in theory to exactly the same
rations as a truck driver; but in the *Voentorg* or "Military
Store" he frequently can actually get his full allotment of
meat, eggs, and sugar, while the truck driver has to take
substitutes or do without.

Moreover, the wealthier Russians can enliven their diet
with purchases at the Gastronoms, where luxury goods
are sold without ration coupons. There are five such stores
in Kiev, and they were always crowded; but most of the
people came merely to look at the delicacies, not to buy.
A glance at the price tags showed why. Live carp, swim-
ming in an aerated tank, were offered for ninety-five

rubles per kilogram or roughly four dollars a pound. Quail, brought into the store by the Society of Hunters, sold for seventy rubles each; brandy for sixty-five rubles a bottle; chocolate bars, fifty rubles; hard, garlic-flavored sausage, rather like salami, forty rubles for one hundred grams, which means a chunk about three inches long. Siberian crab meat, originally packed for the export market and still labeled in English, was priced at forty-five rubles for a small can.

Since the average workingman earns considerably less than a hundred rubles a week, it was hardly surprising that the turnover in these stores was rather slow. Fresh meat, to cite a typical example, sold in Kiev's largest Gastronom at the rate of only about sixty-five pounds a month. Yet the luxury shops fulfill two important purposes, aside from furnishing dainties for the upper classes. They siphon off a good deal of money, which might otherwise exert an inflationary pressure. And, as the manager of one Gastronom told me, they "show the people that good things actually exist—things which everybody can have some day, if we all work hard enough."

For the present, however, not even the privileged groups are well enough fed to prevent all grumbling. In Kharkov the head clerk in an army officers' ration store inquired anxiously whether UNRRA was going to step up its shipments of lard and butter. "We have had many unpleasant incidents in this shop lately," he said. "The soldiers just back from Germany get angry when we aren't able to give them their full ration of fats."

In clothing, as in food, the Soviet class distinctions are plainly marked. The best-dressed men in Russia are the officers of the NKVD troops and the Red Army; their well-fitted uniforms frequently are made of American woolens, supplied under Lend-Lease during the war. In spite of the leather shortage each of them wears excellent knee-high boots, and many are equipped with heavy ankle-length leather overcoats, each containing enough material to make shoes for a dozen barefoot peasants.

Even among civilians the sartorial tradition of the early revolutionary days—when no good Bolshevik would have dreamed of appearing in public wearing a necktie or with creases in his trousers—has almost entirely disappeared. The ruling class now makes little pretense of dressing like the common people. Instead of overalls, a decorous, rather stiffly-cut suit of black or gray is now considered the proper garb for a rising bureaucrat, and I knew one bright young administrator in Poltava who was inordinately proud of his tight, double-breasted overcoat with velvet collar. Even on the collective farms the Party officials and managerial personnel usually can be spotted at a glance, because their clothing is both tidier and of better quality than that of the ordinary peasants.

One lingering trace of the old tradition is the cloth workingman's cap, hallowed by Lenin and therefore still widely popular. Khrushchev had one specially tailored of cream-colored linen, which he wore with a matching suit when he reviewed the May Day parade. The snap-brim felt hat is gaining favor, however. Frequently it is worn without dents in the crown.

Among women a hat of any kind is a sure sign of a high income; the less well off wear shawls or handkerchiefs knotted around their heads. (When a Russian newspaperman was trying to describe to me how prosperous the country was before the war, he summed it up by saying: "Why, in 1940 a great many women already were beginning to wear hats.") The more modish ladies—university students, translators, journalists, doctors—also wear rayon stockings, and most of them make generous use of the lipsticks and other cosmetics which are now back in a few of the luxury stores in fair supply. They get no cold cream, however, because of the fat shortage. Beauty shops and manicurists are heavily patronized, as are the barbers—who are still known by the old czarist name of "peruke maker."

Styles in the outside world are a matter of avid interest. The assistant manager of the hotel where we stayed in Kiev—a pretty twenty-four-year-old widow who had earned two medals as a machine gunner at Stalingrad— picked up a little pin money by dressmaking in her spare time. She was overjoyed at the gift of an old copy of *Life* magazine, which immediately established her as a minor fashion authority. The three American women working with the mission underwent endless questioning about their clothes.

Because of the extreme housing shortage, only the very highest officials enjoy homes which a middle-class American family would consider really adequate. Even those in the middle range of the bureaucracy, however, usually manage to get quarters which are considerably more spacious and comfortable than working-class apartments or peasant huts. A fair sample was the home of Mrs. Nina Gregorievna Parkhomenko at 121 Gogol Street, Zaporozhe, where I stayed as a guest for a few nights. (The Germans had destroyed all the city's hotels.) Her family definitely was in the upper brackets of both rank and income; Mrs. Parkhomenko was an economist and her husband an engineer who was away on an out-of-town construction job at the time of my visit.

Their home was a tidy little cottage with four rooms, two on either side of a central corridor. At one end of the corridor was the front door; at the other a space about four feet square had been partitioned off to form a bathroom. This was equipped with a china washbasin, a tin dishpan for stand-up sponge bathing, and a bucket of water. There was no mirror or plumbing; the water came from a main-line tap standing in the front yard, and the slops were tossed into the garden. A privy of the standard Arkansas type stood at the end of the yard, which was neatly laid out with vegetable patches, fruit trees, and a few beehives.

The four rooms normally accommodated the Parkhomenkos, their fourteen-year-old daughter, and Mrs. Parkhomenko's parents, a well-preserved old couple who did most of the housekeeping and gardening. They put me in the dining room, which was furnished with an iron cot, an old but sturdy table, three chairs, and a china cupboard containing about a dozen inexpensive plates and saucers. On the walls were the inevitable pictures of Stalin and Lenin, plus—an unusual touch—a crayon drawing of a voluptuous lady with a pompadour hair-do and a costume of about 1890. It might have been sketched by Charles Dana Gibson.

The walls had been freshly whitewashed, inside and out; the floor was well scrubbed; and the windows were covered with cheesecloth screening. Moreover, the household had one rare luxury, a piano. It took up a large part of the main bedroom, and as soon as school was out every afternoon the daughter went doggedly to work on Schirmer's five-finger exercises and "The Moonlight Sonata."

The Parkhomenko family considered themselves very lucky, as indeed they were. Their only war damage had been a few panes of glass broken by a distant bomb explosion. Because of their position they had not been required to double up with other families who had lost their homes. They ate relatively well, and might have eaten better if they had been a little less softhearted. In a chicken-wire pen just outside the front door they had six plump rabbits. "Even though we never get enough meat," the grandmother explained, "we can't bear to kill them. They are so gentle and furry."

Even the little amenities are carefully hoarded for distribution as rewards to the deserving. Consequently, ordinary citizens frequently find it hard to buy tickets to the opera or one of the better theaters; many of the seats are reserved for officialdom, military heroes, distinguished visitors, and groups of factory workers who have excelled in the latest output competition. In the Kiev opera house the first six rows usually were allotted almost solidly to officers of the rank of colonel or higher and their wives. The best box was permanently reserved for Khrushchev, although no one knew how often he used it; heavy red velvet drapes screened it off from the rest of the audience, so that no would-be assassin could tell whether or not The Boss was present. (This precaution is not as extreme as it sounds. Thirty-six years ago Prime Minister Peter Stolypin was murdered by a young revolutionist in that same box.)

A similar useful little privilege is the 40 per cent discount at all Gastronom stores which is extended to three classes of customers: generals, the owners of medals won in battle, and factory workmen who have been employed for six consecutive years in the same shop. A ten per cent discount also is provided for office workers who stick for six years. Such incentives help combat the excessive labor turnover, which still is one of Russia's most persistent economic headaches.

Automobiles, telephones, typewriters, air travel, and First Category train accommodations are other items which are largely reserved for allocation to the higher ranks of the bureaucracy and military. I heard of a few individuals—Alexei Tolstoy and other wealthy writers—who owned private cars, but I never met one. In the Ukraine autos were so scarce, in fact, that only Khrushchev and one or two of his top associates had bulletproof Cadillacs assigned for their exclusive use; lower-ranking cabinet members had to depend on a motor pool. Moreover, well above half of the passenger cars I saw in the Ukraine were of German make. They took a terrific beating on the primitive roads, and often were out of service because German spare parts were not readily available.

Social distinctions, as well as creature comforts, indicate plainly the various gradations in the Soviet class structure. Most Russians have a strong sense of hierarchy —a hangover, no doubt, from the centuries of czarist feudalism—and each is quite aware of his place in the social scale. Toward his betters he shows a deferential (though by no means fawning) respect; and he expects the same deference from his inferiors. This attitude crops up in countless little things—the seating arrangement at meals, including even the most informal picnics; who goes through a door first; the special waiting rooms at airports and railway stations for Very Important People; the degree of snappiness in a traffic cop's salute; a tone of voice. It was always easy, for instance, to spot the senior Party member in the welcoming committee as soon as we arrived in any village. He did most of the talking, rode in the leading automobile, and made all the arrangements. Somebody always helped him with his overcoat, and everybody laughed merrily at his little jokes.

As in any community, someone occasionally permitted his sense of social superiority to degenerate into arrogance. Such a case was a minor official who accompanied us on one long journey through the central Ukraine. He suffered from a chronic officiousness which promptly earned him, among the Americans, the nickname of Little Rollo. He embarrassed us constantly by demanding special favors— "We must have two large bouquets on this table immediately"—and by barking orders at everybody from railway conductors to mayors. Instances of this kind were rare, however. Most Russians of rank treated their subordinates with an easy consideration which would have done credit to the British gentry.

This does not mean, however, that they ever encouraged anyone to forget his place. Late one evening, after a hard day of tramping over collective farms, we stopped our jeeps at a little restaurant in the village of Brovary. A few local officials, including the county secretary of the Communist Party, joined us for a snack and a drop of vodka. One toast led to another, and before long everybody was singing Ukrainian folk songs and Texas cowboy ballads; the difference in languages didn't seem, at the moment, to offer any difficulty. Eventually two waitresses—first-rate sopranos—pulled up chairs and joined in. Then one of the Americans suggested that the cooks and dishwashers, who had gathered at the kitchen door, ought to join the chorus, too. That idea was vetoed, promptly and firmly, by the Party secretary. As we left, an hour or so later, he explained with a faint note of apology that singing with waitresses was perfectly okay; but no kitchen help. I never quite got the reason for the distinction, but there was no doubt that it was there.

A less puzzling exhibition of rank occurred in our Kiev hotel when the manager had to move a college professor out of his regular room in order to accommodate a delegation of twenty visiting Yugoslavs all on the same floor. The professor objected, in a thundering basso which carried throughout the building. Our translator gave us a running account as he cursed the hotel, the manager, the impending Yugoslav invasion, and the incredible disrespect being shown to a man of learning. He added that a chambermaid had entered his room without knocking that very morning, and threatened to bring down the discipline of Higher Authority on the whole uncultured establishment. The diatribe went on for forty-five minutes, while the manager made placating gestures and the other guests listened in the corridors. In the end he agreed to move temporarily to another room—somewhat mollified, as I got it, by the argument that some of the Yugoslavs also were professors of distinguished standing.

In passing, it is noteworthy that military men rank significantly lower in the Soviet hierarchy than the civilian authorities, and this fact is made plain to everybody. On holidays, when portraits of the nation's leaders are displayed on giant billboards throughout every city, the pictures of the marshals and generals invariably are smaller than those of the Politburo members, and they are placed in subordinate positions. So with the other standard indications of status—the seating on reviewing stands, the order in which names are published in the newspapers, and the amount of applause indicated in the published accounts of speeches. The text of one of Stalin's talks, for example, is normally interlarded with parenthetical comments: "Stormy, unabating applause, rising to an ovation." A speech by Molotov, say, or Zhdanov is reported as receiving only "stormy, prolonged applause," while a general merely gets "prolonged applause" with nothing stormy about it. Every shrewd Soviet citizen (and foreign diplomat) watches such barometers of rank attentively. A mere shift in precedence in the listing of Party committeemen often gives the surest indication of whose star is rising or which official has fallen into disfavor at court.

Most Moscow diplomats, incidentally, believe that there is scant probability of a serious split between the Party and the Red Army, even at the delicate moment of Stalin's death. The army, they have concluded, is so completely subordinated to the Party, so thoroughly saturated at all levels with NKVD men and political organizers, that an opposition movement would have little chance to develop unnoticed. After all, Laurenti Beria, boss of the political police, holds—among other titles—the rank of marshal in the Red Army.

There are two kinds of class distinction which persist, for the time being, in spite of governmental disapproval. One of them is anti-Semitism, especially in the Ukraine and (I am told) in Byelo-Russia. These were the main areas of Jewish settlement under the czarist regime, and race prejudice had been endemic there for generations. During the occupation it was greatly inflamed by Nazi propaganda, plus certain curious economic pressures. For instance, hundreds of thousands of Jewish families fled east before the invaders, leaving most of their property locked in their homes. Just before the Reichswehr entered a locality, these abandoned houses frequently were broken open and plundered by the Ukrainians who had not been evacuated. ("If we don't take it, the Germans will.") At the end of the war the looters feared, naturally enough, that

the Jews would return and claim their property, perhaps
bringing criminal charges as well, and as a result the first
of the homecoming refugees encountered a good deal of
open hostility. Some anti-Semitism was still evident nearly
two years later, but it was no longer virulent and the government was making a quiet but earnest effort to combat
it. I heard of one Jewish lawyer, a prosecuting attorney
before the war, who asked for his old job back when he
got out of the Red Army. A representative of the Council
of Ministers turned him down, with this explanation:

"We have to prosecute a lot of collaborators and
traitors. If you handled the job it might start a lot of
rumors about the Jews trying to take revenge. It would
be smarter for you to serve as a defense attorney for a few
months. Then, when the collaboration cases are finished,
we'll take you back on the prosecutor's staff."

Despite such apparently sincere efforts to damp down
racial feeling among the masses, there are some indications
of racial discrimination within the ruling class itself. I did
not encounter a single Jew in the upper ranks of the
Ukrainian bureaucracy, although a considerable part of
the republic's population is Jewish; and a few minor Jewish
officials hinted that they encountered some prejudice
among their Ukrainian colleagues. Only one Jew—Kaganovich—sits on the Politburo. In recent years, moreover,
Jews have been barred from recruitment into the Soviet
foreign service, in which they once predominated because
of their knowledge of foreign languages and the outside
world.

Several Soviet citizens told me that they believed the

reason for this high-level anti-Semitism runs back to the great struggle for power between Stalin and Trotsky. Not only Trotsky himself but many of his closest allies in the original 1924 clash were Jewish; and during the 1937 purge many other Jews, previously unsuspect, were executed as Trotskyites or Zinovievites. Since that date Stalin has seemed reluctant to entrust Jews with positions of power. I heard estimates that as high as eighty per cent of the Jews in the Party had been dropped from membership in the last two years. The discrimination in the foreign service may, of course, be partly due to a belief that anti-Semitic feeling abroad might handicap a Jewish diplomat.

A special class of quite a different kind is the speculators. They are enterprising (but perhaps foolhardy) people who make a business of traveling through rural areas to buy up meat, eggs, and other surplus food for resale in the "free" markets which were described in Chapter III. Here they frequently barter the farm produce for secondhand clothing or household goods, which they then trade off to the peasants on their next trip to the country—making profits ranging up to several hundred per cent on both ends of the swap. This business—sometimes supplemented with a little black-marketing in German war booty—has proved so lucrative that the speculators have become a small but well-defined new-rich group. Their rather blatant prosperity has aroused a good deal of resentment among peasants and city people alike.

Private speculation of this sort is, of course, a screaming violation of Communist principles. It is tolerated, for the moment, because the normal machinery of food distribution was crippled by the war. Until this machinery can be rebuilt, the speculators provide a stopgap, unsatisfactory and even wicked by the Soviet moral code, but better than none at all. It is a safe bet that they will be suppressed as "enemies of the people" as soon as the government feels it can manage without them.

The obvious differences in rank and privileges throughout the USSR do not budge for an instant the Communist's conviction that he is living in a classless society. He can always fall back on the argument that no ruling group controls the instruments of production. Even this argument, however, is a little hard for the non-Marxist mind to follow.

The Russian Communist Party, as we have seen, constitutes a small, tightly knit, self-perpetuating elite—"people of a special mold," in Stalin's phrase. It bears all of the customary stigmata of a governing class. It also controls the instruments of production as completely as any ruling class in history.

It alone decides what use shall be made of land, factories, labor, and raw materials; and no other ruling group in modern society can make such decisions with so little regard for the desires of the rest of the community. The managers of American industry are subject to constant pressure from both labor and consumers, but Soviet management has no need to pay much attention to either. Russian trade unions, as we shall note in a later chapter, have far less voice in management than their American counterparts. They can neither strike, bargain for higher wages, nor demand shorter hours. In many cases they have not even been able to compel plant managers to pay wages which were months overdue. Nor can the consumer influence production policy except in the most feeble and indirect manner; by and large, he takes whatever his bosses please to give him.

The Communists insist that they do not use the land and factories under their control for personal profit; but this seems to be little more than a quibble over wording. Certainly they enjoy all the perquisites in prestige and higher living standards which are commonly associated with ownership. It would be illuminating to discover whether a higher percentage of the national income goes to the managing and investing groups in America than goes to the bureaucracy in Russia, but the secrecy hiding nearly all Soviet statistics prevents such a comparison.

The Soviet dictatorship professes, of course, to be merely a kind of self-appointed trustee, using its power and resources in the long-run interest of all the people. The same claim has been made by every ruling class. It was the chief justification of the feudal nobility; on these very grounds Charles II defended the divine right of kings; Adam Smith made the same point in his classic argument for capitalism. The dominant aristocracy in Russia or anywhere else almost automatically identifies its interest with the interest of the state, and comes to regard its special privileges as a just payment for the arduous duties of management. It has also been standard procedure for almost every ruling clique which is not directly responsible to public opinion to devote a large share of the resources it controls to war preparations. Here, again, the Russians are following the normal pattern.

It might be expected, from the previous performance of such groups, that the Communist Party eventually will tend to become a hereditary governing elite, much like the German Junkers or the upper middle class of Victorian England. The regime is still too young, of course, for such a tendency to develop very far, but there are a few indications that it may be in the bud. The children of Soviet officials naturally find it easier to attain the coveted Party membership card which is the passport to positions of authority. They also manage, in many cases, to wangle choice assignments—not through bald nepotism, but simply because they are known and trusted by papa's good friend on the local council. (One of my Ukrainian friends told me with some pride how he was trying to make just such an arrangement for a young woman doctor who was engaged to his son. She wanted a job in Kiev, rather than in some remote village, and my friend, who was an influential Party member, put in a word at the right moment with the Minister of Health.)

Even higher education is tending to become a prerogative of the wealthy and influential since the introduction —a few years ago—of tuition fees in the universities and technical institutes. These fees are not high, and they are supplemented by scholarships for poor but deserving students. Yet they weigh the scales very considerably in favor of the children of prosperous (which usually means Communist Party) families. And a university or technical degree is becoming more and more indispensable for advancement in the professions and the bureaucracy.

Here and there the habits of ostentatious display and conspicuous waste, which Veblen has noted as the classic earmarks of a hereditary leisure class, already are beginning to crop up. They show in the mink coats and silver fox capes which generals' wives sometimes wear to chamber music concerts, and in the expensive perfumes offered in the big city luxury shops. They are perhaps most noticeable in Moscow's three swanky hot spots—the Cocktail Hall on Gorki Street, the Aurora Café, and the Moscow Hotel bar. Cocktail Hall is a faithful imitation of a New York night club, complete with glittery décor, circular bar, and a sleek female crooner. It is frequented largely by young people, obviously well endowed, who pay $7.50 for a cocktail made of vodka and grenadine syrup. Such gaudy behavior is still too rare, however, to have much significance—except as a straw in the wind.

In the long run the survival of the Communist hierarchy may well depend upon its ability to confine the inheritance of power within reasonable limits and to keep on absorbing new blood from the lower classes. Failure to solve this problem of renewal probably was a major cause of the decline of the Prussian Junkers and the Two Hundred Families of France. Conversely, the extraordinary willingness of the British ruling class to accept rising young men from below perhaps accounts in part for its persistent vitality, even under a Labor government. The present leaders of the Communist Party are, I believe, quite aware of the historic gravity of this problem. Whether their successors will forget it, as the czars did, is a question which can hardly be answered short of two or three generations.

A final footnote on the classless society might well be provided by the chorus girl mentioned at the beginning of this chapter. She could have argued, with approximate accuracy, that there are no prostitutes in the Soviet Union, for she and some hundreds of other women belong in quite a different category. They might almost be described as Communist geisha girls.

By a combination of measures—heavy punishment for streetwalking, encouragement of early marriage, and putting women to work in less traditional fields—the government has virtually wiped out commercial prostitution. It permits certain exceptions, however, as an aid in its handling of foreigners.

Among the strangers whom it has to put up with, however reluctantly, there are always a few unattached males, mostly diplomats, newspapermen, and merchant seamen calling at Russian ports. It is a settled policy to keep all contact between foreigners and the Soviet people within rigidly controlled limits, so the government takes no chance on these foot-loose men striking up random acquaintances with native women. Instead it has designated certain small groups—notably ballerinas, actresses, the secretaries of correspondents, and some Intourist guides —who are permitted to fraternize with foreigners. Most of the resulting friendships are entirely respectable. If a cozier relationship occasionally develops, however, the police tactfully overlook it.

One result is what Moscow correspondents describe as The Chocolate Bar Circuit. This is a group of shapely and cordial young ladies who hang around the Metropole Hotel and the adjoining opera-house square. They show a lively gratitude for the chocolate bars, soap, nylon stockings, and similar exotic gifts which foreigners billeted at the Metropole often are in a position to provide. Some of them have even been known to accept a fur coat. Unlike most Soviet citizens, they are not difficult to get to know. The standard technique is to buy a pair of opera tickets and then stroll around the little park in front of the Bolshoi Theater a few minutes before curtain time. One of those inviting blondes, who by coincidence happens to be strolling there at the same hour, almost certainly will be glad to share the tickets with you.

A similar group provides diversion for the sailors who put up at the Intourist Hotel in Odessa; they are reputed to wear the shortest skirts in the Soviet Union. I have been told that their counterparts can be found in Leningrad, Murmansk, and Archangel.

It is commonly supposed among foreigners in Russia that these young ladies have close working relationships with the NKVD. I never heard any conclusive evidence on this point. An incident which occurred the first time I went to the ballet in Kiev may, however, have some pertinence. I was accompanied that night by Pavel Petrovich Purobayev, an English-speaking NKVD man who later became one of my warmest acquaintances in the

Ukraine. At the end of the first act he inquired whether I liked the girls. I told him, quite truthfully, that they looked pretty wonderful.

"Pick out the one you would like to meet, then," Pavel said. "I arrange everything."

I'm still sorry that the decorum which our mission imposed on all of us prevented me from taking up his offer. I am confident that both his intentions and the ballerinas were morally above reproach.

CHAPTER
SIX
THE BIG PRIZE

THAT PERSUASIVE COMBINATION OF THE COOKIE and The Whip is not applied to the individual Soviet citizen alone. In their efforts to discipline the unruly and hustle the laggards, the men in the Kremlin occasionally mete out rewards and penalties to whole nationalities. The Oriental tradition of group responsibility is deeply embedded in the Russian mind; the Western notion that a man is responsible only for his own actions, and not for those of his relatives and neighbors, has never gained much acceptance.

One example of group punishment is the barrier against Jews in the bureaucracy which was mentioned in the last chapter. Better known is the case of the five "autonomous" republics which were abolished soon after the end of the war because considerable numbers of their people had sided with the German invaders. Two of these—the Crimean and the Chechen-Ingush Republics—not only were reduced to the status of provinces; many thousands of their inhabitants also were exiled to remote sections of Siberia, as part of a systematic plan to blot out these stubborn and unreliable nationalities entirely. They were

mostly Moslems who had never been wholly reconciled
to Soviet rule, and during the war they had—in the words
of the official decree of punishment—"formed diversion
bands for a struggle with Soviet power in the rear" and
had joined the Nazis to wage "an armed struggle against
units of the Red Army."

On the other hand, the Kremlin has from time to time
conferred blanket rewards on nationalities it considers
particularly deserving. The biggest prize of this kind was
its grant of "independence" to the Ukraine and to Byelo-
Russia ,which up until February 1, 1944, had been on the
same footing as the rest of the sixteen Union Republics.
A constitutional amendment of that date—which in theory
applies to all Union Republics but in practice only to these
two—ostensibly gave them many of the privileges of full-
fledged nations. They acquired the right to set up their
own foreign ministries, send diplomats abroad, and maintain their own military units. Most important of all, they
were qualified for admission to the United Nations as
"sovereign and independent states."

At the time it was widely assumed in the outside world
that this grant of independence was simply an elaborate
Communist maneuver to get a couple of extra votes in the
United Nations. No doubt those two votes had something
to do with it, but they are by no means the whole explanation. Few things in Russia are ever that simple.

A much weightier reason, I am convinced, was the
eagerness of the Politburo to bestow some spectacular reward upon these two bruised, proud, and restive republics.
They had absorbed the main impact of the German inva-

sion. They had suffered the most grievous losses in blood and property. Moreover, the Ukrainians especially had cherished for generations a strong nationalist sentiment, which was methodically encouraged by the Germans during the occupation. (Sometimes such propaganda had unlooked-for results. I was told that certain guerrilla bands which called themselves "Green Guards" sprang up in 1942 and 1943. They fought both the Reichswehr and the Red Army in hopes of establishing a free Ukrainian nation—just as similar bands under Nestor Makhno had done during the years of the Revolution and civil war. Some remnants were said to be still living in the woods and supporting themselves by banditry as late as the spring of 1946 under the leadership of a legendary character known as Stepan Bandera.)

An award of nominal independence obviously was the easiest way to satisfy—or, at least, to salve—this inflamed nationalist feeling. It could not be forcibly suppressed, as it was in Crimea, simply because the Ukraine and Byelo-Russia were too big and too important. Consequently, Stalin told Roosevelt at their Yalta meeting that he wanted to seat these two republics in the United Nations "for internal political reasons." And Roosevelt, who was always sympathetic to a plea of this kind from one practical politician to another, eventually agreed.

Stalin may also have figured that this step would help solve a minor but irritating problem which grew out of Russia's wartime conquests. The new territories taken over from Poland, Rumania, and Czechoslovakia contained several million people who were Ukrainian by

speech and heritage; but not all of these were wildly enthusiastic about becoming Soviet subjects. Some two hundred thousand, indeed, fled toward western Europe and
have doggedly resisted every effort to force them to return. Other thousands who did not flee still nursed the
old, glowing dream of a separate Ukrainian nation, which
has never quite died since the legendary days of Mazeppa
and Khmelnitzky. If these reluctant newcomers could be
offered citizenship in a Ukrainian Republic which had
some color of independence, it seemed probable that they
would accept the new regime a little less grudgingly.

(The Kremlin may be planning to use the same technique elsewhere one of these days. The Armenian Soviet
Republic recently set up its own foreign ministry and
seems to be moving quietly toward a quasi-independent
status much like that of the Ukraine. It borders on the
territory which Russia would like to "liberate" from
Turkey. No well-schooled Communist would be surprised if a movement should develop within the next year
or two—spontaneously, of course—to unite the Armeni-
ans on both sides of the border in an enlarged and independent Armenian state.)

How well has the Kremlin's gift of independence served
its purpose? And what did the Ukrainians really get?

As a sop to nationalist feeling, it apparently is working
pretty well—though by no means perfectly. Most of the
Ukrainians I met were proudly conscious of their country's
new stature, and they took a grateful, almost childlike joy
in their trappings of sovereignty. When our UNRRA

mission arrived in Kiev, for example, the welcoming delegation included an assistant minister from the fledgling
Ukrainian Foreign Ministry, resplendent in a tight-
waisted gray uniform with silver shoulder boards and a
gray Persian lamb hat. He greeted us, somewhat euphe-
mistically, as "the first foreign ambassadors to the
Ukraine." (We did have a sort of jackleg diplomatic
status, but we were hardly as grand as all that.) Another
official who escorted us a little later to our office—a comfortable, neatly remodeled seven-room dwelling—explained that it had not been prepared for our use alone.
"After you leave," he said, "there will be many diplomats
coming to Kiev, and this will no doubt serve as one of the
legations."

We heard frequent mention of "the Ukrainian ambassadors"—a term which puzzled me until I learned that
it was a rather wistful courtesy title conferred on the republic's permanent representatives in Moscow. They
actually were liaison men handling day-to-day dealings
with the central government; but they were the nearest
thing to ambassadors that the Ukraine had. A more satisfactory symbol of national pride was Dmitri Manuilsky,
the republic's brisk and bouncy foreign minister, a sort
of Fiorello La Guardia character. It was generally felt that
his fiery speeches before the United Nations were making
the rest of the world sit up and take notice.

The great majority of Ukrainians seemed to feel that
they now have about all the independence and recognition
they want. If any large-scale separatist movement still
exists, I could find no hint of it. Yet there are enough

scattered, smouldering embers to cause the Party bosses considerably anxiety. One of my friends spoke repeatedly of the "many, many bad people" who had been misled by the Germans and were "waiting for a chance to cause trouble." (He was an NKVD man, so he should know.) The Party headquarters in Odessa was destroyed in the winter of 1945 by a fire which, according to common gossip, had been started by such malcontents. Latent hostility among the peasants was strong enough to move the *Bolshevik*, leading Party political magazine, to publish a warning against "backward elements" among the farmers in the formerly occupied areas "in whose consciousness survivals of private ownership are still strong." There were also reports that certain officials quite high in the local bureaucracy felt that the Ukraine had carried more than its share of the war burden, and was not getting enough help toward reconstruction from the rest of the USSR. How accurate these stories may be, I have no way to judge. But I did note that some Party members hardly bothered to conceal their feeling of superiority, occasionally tinged with contempt, toward their colleagues from other regions. And there were traces of resentment because so many key jobs were filled by "foreigners."

The Ukrainian Communists have, indeed, always been regarded as mavericks who do not quite merit the full trust of the Kremlin. The last of the native political bosses— Bondarenko, Postichev, Kossior, and Lubchenko—were eliminated in the Great Purge of 1937, and the Politburo sent in an outsider, Nikita Khrushchev, to run both the Party and the government of the Ukraine. Manuilsky and several other of his chief lieutenants also are non-Ukrainians. They are still having troubles with a persistent nationalist feeling among their native subordinates. In an effort to root it out, Khrushchev conducted a drastic purge in the summer of 1946 of all those suspected of "idealizing the past" and attempting "to give rebirth to bourgeois-nationalistic conceptions." This housecleaning —according to Khrushchev's own figures—swept out sixty-four per cent of all the regional Party chairmen and thirty-eight per cent of the regional secretaries. In the machine tractor stations, which are the main tool for controlling the peasantry, two-thirds of the directors had to be replaced. It is perhaps significant that so many Ukrainian Communists turned out to be unreliable, after twenty-eight years of Soviet training.

The 1946 purge was the most telling indication of how much independence the Ukraine actually has. It made plain the fact—if anyone ever doubted it—that the republic is still under the absolute political domination of Moscow. A word from the Politburo can still break any Ukrainian office holder, down to the most obscure village tractor manager.

In cultural matters, however, the Ukrainians are permitted a little more elbow room. One of the Soviet Union's most loudly proclaimed glories is, of course, the "cultural autonomy" granted to each of its many nationalities; so the Ukrainians are encouraged to use their own language and to develop their own music, drama, and literature. Within limits, naturally.

The language, for instance, is taught in the schools on a parity with Russian. The lower grades often have two teachers, one speaking Ukrainian and the other Russian, so that their pupils grow up completely bilingual. Local papers are printed in Ukrainian, along with a number of current novels and books of poetry, and the larger cities usually have at least one native-language theater.

Yet there is something a little affected and unreal about it, like the hothouse cultivation of Gaelic in Ireland. Almost never did we hear Ukrainian spoken on the streets of Kiev. Now and then we came across a shop with a Ukrainian sign, but both clerks and customers spoke Russian as a matter of course. In the remoter villages Ukrainian was more common, but even there the bureaucrats and the better-educated young people usually made a point of speaking Russian. We finally got the impression that, although the language was ostensibly encouraged, it was also subtly made to appear a little countrified and unfashionable.

About the only people who seemed to take it really seriously were the poets. They regarded themselves as the heirs of the great Shevchenko, the Ukrainian Bobby Burns, and they couldn't quite understand why his work and their own was not more widely appreciated in the western world. One of Kiev's most distinguished poets was hotly indignant because American publishers had shown no interest in translating his books.

"We've translated Shakespeare into Ukrainian," he said. "It would only be fair, wouldn't it, for them to publish my work in English?"

He also was astounded to hear that in America verse writing is not a particularly lucrative profession, for in the Ukraine poets are respected and prosperous pillars of society. There is nothing obscure or arty about their product; it is mostly of the boy-stood-on-the-burning-deck or thin-red-line-of-heroes variety, and its frank purpose is to inspire patriotism and glorify the Soviet Fatherland. During the war many poets traveled like troubadours from village to village behind the German lines, reciting their verses to encourage resistance to the invaders.

The Ukrainian theater is far less political—or at least it was during the time I worked there. It is true that the native choruses, which can sing circles around any other choir or glee club I ever heard, concentrate on patriotic songs, but the opera, ballet, and drama were in quite a different tradition. The two most popular operas were *Natalka Poltavka*, which might be translated as "Natalie from Poltava," and *Zaporozhets za Dunayem*, or "The Cossacks on the Danube," both written long before the Revolution. They are light operas, not very different from "Blossom Time" or "The Student Prince." The first concerns a peasant girl whose childhood lover has gone off to seek his fortune, and who is being forced by her mother into marriage with a rich but elderly village squire. The lover, fortunately, returns in the nick of time. The other is a costume number about a band of Cossacks who settled long ago in Turkish territory, and their efforts to persuade the sultan to let them return home. Both are generously laced with slapstick, of about the same delicacy and ideological content as an American burlesque show.

Bucolic love and foot-stomping melodrama of the *East Lynne* brand were favorite themes in the native-language plays, and the ballet was similarly nonpolitical. *The Forest Song*, a new Ukrainian ballet which was first performed in Kiev while I was there, was full of dryads, sprites, and wood nymphs who apparently had never heard of Karl Marx.

Many productions of this sort reportedly were swept off the stage, however, in the nation-wide purge of the arts which got under way in the fall of 1946. Presumably they were among the "erroneous, empty works deprived of ideology and of no value" which were denounced at that time by the Communist Central Committee. It shook up the administration of the entire Russian theater, warned playwrights, poets, and novelists to "improve their unsatisfactory work," and bluntly directed that future productions must "propagandize actively the policy of the Soviet state." Within the limits of this directive, Russian artists enjoy complete freedom, of course, just as the American Tobacco Company advertising men are permitted a wide choice of adjectives in praising Lucky Strike cigarettes. The main difference is that the Soviet writer can't switch to another account.

The nearest thing to real independence and virility in Ukrainian culture probably is the Orthodox Church. It not only has survived two decades of suppression and antireligious propaganda; it even seemed to thrive under persecution, as Christian churches have done before.

In the end the Politburo finally remembered that venerable political maxim, "If you can't lick 'em, join 'em," and shortly before the beginning of the war it made a deal with the priesthood. The Church promised to give its wholehearted support to the Soviet regime, and in return the government shut off its antireligious propaganda, disbanded the League of Militant Atheists, reopened some eight thousand churches, authorized the training of priests in theological seminaries, and permitted believers to worship unmolested.

In the Ukraine the response surprised even the clergy, and I have been told that much the same thing happened in other parts of Russia. People flocked back into the arms of the Church literally by the millions. For example, at St. Vladimir's Cathedral, three blocks from my hotel in Kiev, Sunday services had to be run off in relays from daybreak to dusk in order to accommodate all of the worshipers. On Easter morning the cathedral was packed to the doors before dawn, and some four thousand people stood on the grounds outside. Many of them had brought cakes or loaves of bread to be blessed, and they waited quietly for hours while the priests made their way through the crowd, sprinkling a few drops of holy water on each loaf. These were not merely old folks or unenlightened peasants; they were of all ages and classes, many of them well dressed and obviously prosperous. Among them were a number of Red Army officers, ranging in rank up to full colonel. A few policemen were on hand to see that nobody got hurt in the crush, but they did not interfere in any way with the ceremonies.

The Church's influence shows up in many little ways.

I noted that even the smallest children, for instance, invariably took off their caps when they entered a church. Visiting priests from the Carpathians were assigned choice rooms in Kiev's best hotel. Salaries range from three thousand rubles a month for a village priest to forty thousand for top bishops. The Germans' wanton destruction of the once-lovely Lavra monastery caused more indignation than almost any other outrage in Kiev, and an inspection of its ruins climaxed the official sight-seeing tour on our first day in the city. The sixty monks still living at Lavra—grave, bearded men in ankle-length blue denim robes and conical fur hats—had been driven away by the Germans but were welcomed back by the Red Army as soon as it recaptured the city. Everyone, including the police and Party officials, treated them with respectful courtesy.

The Church is now serving as a useful instrument of Soviet foreign policy among the Orthodox Slavs of eastern Europe. For example, Bishop Eliterios, a Soviet citizen from Rostov, recently was installed as head of the Orthodox Congregations in Czechoslovakia. Both at home and abroad, of course, it operates under strict government supervision. (The administrative control of religious affairs is vested in a special bureau of the NKVD, irreverently nicknamed "The God Office.") Yet the Church has not become a mere tool of the state, like most other Russian institutions. On the contrary, church and government are by no means entirely reconciled. Officially religion is still regarded as a deplorable superstition, and no churchgoer can ever hope to gain admittance to the Communist

Party. The clergy, on the other hand, preach a spiritual faith which is fundamentally at odds with Marxist materialism. Their very existence is a standing challenge to the doctrine that all wisdom and moral authority rest in the Party.

The leaders of the Church, moreover, are virtually the only men of outstanding ability who have not been absorbed into the machinery of the government. Like the early Bolsheviks, they learned to flourish under oppression, and in the process they acquired a political schooling which cannot be bought in any other way. At the same time, the priesthood was cleansed of all but its staunchest, bravest, and most dedicated men.

As a result, the Church today possesses the only reservoir of political talent outside the Communist Party and is the only non-Party organization capable of reaching any considerable number of the Russian people. If the power of the Communists should ever crumble as the result of some future war or (highly unlikely) internal discord, the Orthodox Church might then prove to be the only source capable of supplying a new leadership.

In economic matters, I found no pretense that the Ukraine had any independence whatever. It is tightly fitted into the Five Year Plan, just like every other section of the USSR, and nobody in the Ukraine has authority to shift the site or the production goals of a single major factory. In many cases, in fact, we discovered that the Ukrainian government did not even keep separate statistics on local output and stocks on hand; they were lumped

together with the national totals in the elaborate bookkeeping apparatus of the State Planning Commission in
Moscow.

The new Five Year Plan made unpleasant reading for
Ukrainians. It announced that the republic would have to
give up the industrial leadership it has so long enjoyed
because the Politburo had decided to shift the main centers of heavy industry to new areas beyond the Ural
mountains. The reason is plain enough: the Ukraine is
too close to the western border. In getting ready for the
next war, the government feels it must locate its key factories as far as possible out of reach of bombing planes and
invading armies. "Restriction of the construction of new
industrial plants" also was decreed for Leningrad, Moscow, Rostov, Gorky, and other vulnerable districts.

In the context of over-all Soviet policy, this decision is
simply good sense. But that doesn't make it any more
palatable for the Ukrainians. It may, indeed, have been one
of the incidents behind the recent purge of Ukrainian
office holders, for many of them are incurably saturated
with local pride.

The Ukraine will hold on to a good many of its industries, of course, because it has certain natural resources
which cannot be moved. The water power at the Zaporozhe rapids, to cite the most obvious case, either has to
be used right there or go to waste; so the big Dnieper dam
is being rebuilt, along with the cluster of nearby factories
which depend on its electricity. (A number of them, however, are being changed over to produce consumers' goods
instead of heavy equipment.) Steel mills must be rebuilt

to use the coal in the Donets Basin and the iron ore at Krivoi Rog; thirty blast furnaces and fifty-eight rolling mills are scheduled to be in operation by 1950. Fabricating plants to convert part of the finished steel into railway cars, farm machinery, and mining equipment also will be restored, and The Plan provides for one small automobile factory, capable of turning out about five thousand cars a month.

Most of the redevelopment in the republic, however, will be concentrated on light industries, such as refineries for its sugar beets, canneries, vegetable-oil mills, meat-packing plants, and building-material factories. Machine-tool production, the item marked for the greatest expansion under the Five Year Plan, will be centered elsewhere; of the seventy-four thousand metalworking machine tools scheduled for completion in 1950, less than six thousand will be built in the Ukraine.

If the Ukraine's independence is something less than complete in the fields of politics, culture, and economics, that is all the more reason for keeping the outward symbols of prestige and independence polished as bright as possible. Consequently, the republic often is assigned a leading role among Russia's brood of satellite states, and is given generous opportunities to throw out its chest on the international stage. Manuilsky got the honor of indicting Greece and Great Britain as warmongers before the United Nations, for example, and his speeches often get prominence in the Soviet press second only to Molotov's.

(The Byelo-Russian representatives have been notably less conspicuous in international deliberations, for the Byelo-Russians are a less rambunctious and nationalistic people than the Ukrainians, and carry far less political and economic weight within the Soviet Union. Consequently, the Kremlin sees little reason to butter up their ego.)

Probably it is reasonable to guess that Manuilsky will continue to roar and toss his mane at the United Nations meetings so long as the Politburo is a little uneasy about the state of affairs in the Ukraine. And if he ever sinks into the background, that might be taken as a sign that all is serene again among his folks back home.

CHAPTER
SEVEN

THE BLONDE
FROM DETROIT

THE MIDDLE-AGED WOMAN WITH THE FORLORN, heavy face said she had been born in Detroit, and she wanted to go home. More than anything else in the world, she said, she wanted to get out of Russia. She had come to my hotel room in Kiev to see if I could help.

Sophie Rudenko—that's close enough to her real name—told me her parents were Polish Ukrainians who had emigrated to America in 1900. They had sent her through seven grades of a Catholic parochial school in one of Detroit's drearier suburbs. There she had learned to speak English, with only the softest overtone of a Slavic accent, but it never did come as easily as the Ukrainian she always heard at home. She had worked as a waitress, movie usher, and finally cashier in a small theater before she got married at the age of nineteen. She must have been pretty then, in a strapping, heiferish fashion. (When I met her, she was thirty-nine, according to her passport. Her blonde hair was streaked with gray; she puffed a little climbing the stairs; and her thick ankles were blotched with varicose veins.)

Sophie's husband was a wrestler, also of Eastern European parentage—probably Polish. (On this point her story seemed to vary from time to time. Probably he never was an American citizen.) They had barnstormed around the country wherever he could pick up a match at an Elks' smoker or a country fair. "We did real good at first," she said. "Steve wore silk shirts, got shaved in a barbershop every day, and bought me everything I asked for. But that's a young man's game, and after while it got so he couldn't draw more than maybe fifty or seventy-five bucks for a night's work. We began to save our money and look around for a chance to settle down."

Since they had never made many friends in America—"you just don't, traveling around all the time"—Steve and Sophie got the idea of going to Poland. The few thousand dollars they had saved would be a fortune there, and Steve, the big-shot wrestler, might be something of a hero. Besides, it would be nice to live with their own kind of people; and there didn't seem to be much of a future for a worn-out grunt artist in the United States.

So they went—in the spring of 1939. (Neither of them, apparently, ever read a newspaper.) They opened a little movie theater in a small town near Posen. Sophie sold tickets and Steve ran the projector. They got along fine—until the Germans came.

Then Sophie went to a concentration camp for four months, and after that she was in the hospital for a long time. (Her husband apparently never was imprisoned by the Germans—a circumstance some members of our mission thought a little queer.) The last American repatriation ship left while she was still too ill to travel. Eventually she got well enough to work, and she and Steve got along somehow with a series of odd jobs in Posen until the Red Army captured the city in the closing months of the war.

Because they spoke Ukrainian, the Rudenkos managed to get themselves evacuated to Russia. "We thought any place would be better than Poland in those days." They ended up in Kiev, where Steve had a widowed sister-in-law who took them into her apartment.

"All through the war I had hung onto my American passport," Sophie told me. "But when we got to Kiev the police said I would have to give it up, and that we would have to become Russian citizens. Unless we did, we couldn't get work, and Steve's sister-in-law couldn't feed us for long. Steve finally accepted Soviet citizenship, but he told me to keep my passport no matter what happened, no matter if they threw me in jail. Without it, neither of us would have a chance of getting home again."

Steve was promptly given work as a physical education teacher in a primary school at the relatively good salary of six hundred rubles a month. He didn't get paid for several months, however, because—as Sophie explained it—"they said all Americans were known to be rich, and didn't need the money. Besides, they kept saying they had won the war for us, so we Americans should be glad to work for nothing."

Even after Steve persuaded the government to give him his pay, the Rudenkos found life bitterly hard. The sister-in-law's tiny apartment was crowded with her own children, so that the Americans felt both uncomfortable and unwelcome. They weren't used to living almost entirely on black bread, and Steve didn't earn enough to pay for meat, sunflower-seed oil, or other delicacies in the open markets. About once a month Sophie would trade a piece of their extra clothing for a chunk of sausage or mutton, and they would have a feast.

"But now nearly everything is gone, except what I've got on my back," Sophie said. She was wearing a neat black dress, only a little frayed at the cuffs and elbows, an American-made hat, and a faded black coat with a cheap fur collar. They were shabby but they fitted, so that she still looked better dressed than most of the women in Kiev. She also carried a worn leather purse, which contained her precious passport.

"The worst thing is the loneliness," she said. "Nobody will talk to us. They are all afraid of another purge, and they won't have anything to do with foreigners. Once I thought I had got on friendly terms with a woman I met at the market. But when I tried to visit at her home, she begged me to go away and never come back. She said the police knew everything, and she didn't dare let me in. So now I spend most of my time sitting in the park, when I'm not writing letters."

Sophie wrote a lot of letters, all of them to the American embassy in Moscow. She never got an answer. (Later, when I asked about it at the embassy, I found that none of her letters had ever reached there.) Once she had tried to phone the embassy, to plead for help in getting home, but the telephone office had refused to let her place the long-distance call. She also had tried to go to Moscow to present her case in person, but had not been able to get a permit to buy a railroad ticket.

"I thought of cabling to my relatives in America," Sophie told me, "but Steve's sister-in-law wouldn't let me. She cried and screamed at me and finally threatened to put us out of the apartment if I did it. You see, anybody who sends a telegram has to put a home address at the bottom of the form. And if her address appeared on a cable to America, she didn't know what would happen. She was afraid the police might take her away."

All Sophie wanted me to do was to get word to the embassy about the fix she was in, and to ask somebody to get her out of there.

"I can't stand it much longer," she said. "You don't know what it's like, living among all these down-and-out people, and everybody scared to death all the time. If they won't let my husband leave, I'll go alone—he's agreed that's the best thing to do. Maybe I can do something to help him get away once I'm back in America. But I've got to get out of here soon. You've just got to help me. . . ."

I promised, of course. When I passed through Moscow a couple of months later, I told the whole story to a Foreign Service officer who handled such matters. (Meanwhile, Sophie had come back time after time, begging me and the other members of the UNRRA mission to help her, until we had to warn her for her own sake to stay away from the hotel. Association with other foreigners would, at the very least, have made her case more difficult.)

The Foreign Service officer sighed in a weary kind of way and said he would do what he could.

"But we have more than a thousand cases much like the Rudenkos'," he said, "and so far we haven't had much luck with them. A good many Americans came over here in the ten years before the war because they got excited over the great Russian experiment and wanted to take a part in it. They weren't Communists, most of them—just enthusiastic liberals who had read a lot of the propaganda and had decided that the Soviets were doing something too wonderful to miss.

"They got over that pretty quick, of course, and many of them started trying to get back home after they had worked in Russia just a few weeks. Unfortunately, nearly all had applied for Soviet citizenship before they came, or had given up their passports on arrival. Naturally enough, the Russians won't let them go—they don't like for people who have seen too much of this country to get a chance to talk about it outside. And under the circumstances, the embassy can seldom put on enough pressure to get them an exit permit."

Sophie's story, however, had a happier ending. Months later I learned that she eventually had been able to reach Moscow, obtain an exit permit, and book a passage home.

Life in a police state undoubtedly seemed more disagreeable to Sophie than it does to most Russians. She wasn't used to it, and as a foreigner she naturally got an extra share of attention from the NKVD.

Actually the average Soviet citizen does not regard him-

self as "down and out"—although he may look that way
to anyone accustomed to American living standards—nor
is he "scared to death all the time." If he works hard, keeps
his mouth shut, avoids foreigners, keeps his passport in
order, and does what he is told, he need have no fear of
the secret police. Or, at least, not much. There is always
the chance, of course, that he will be whisked off to a
concentration camp for somebody else's indiscretions,
since innocent people have suffered—by the Soviet government's own admission—in each of the recurrent purges.
Such mishaps are unavoidable, however, in any totalitarian
society; and the individual must always remember that
the state is not run for his convenience but for The Masses.

Moreover, a tightly policed society seems so normal to
most Russians that they can hardly conceive of any other
kind. (They simply did not believe me when I told them,
in response to an occasional question, that the FBI could
not throw a man in jail for criticizing the government,
nor hold him without a public trial.) Political police have
always been a familiar feature of Russian life—perhaps
even an inevitable one, in view of the country's peculiar
geography. Because it is a level, defenseless plain, entic-
ingly open to invaders, no government has ever been able
to survive there for long unless it kept ready for instant
war.

That meant a strong, semimilitary, highly centralized
government. It meant large standing armies and constant
alertness against spies and traitors. It meant compulsory
political unity under something like martial law, with a
political police to enforce it. Under these conditions, such

democratic habits as free discussion, elected governments, guarantees against arbitrary arrest, and trial by jury never had much chance to take root. You can't run an army on that basis; and Russia has always had to be a kind of armed camp.

(A good deal of historical evidence might be marshaled for the argument that civil liberties are delicate growths which seldom flourish without the protection of an ocean moat. They got a firm foothold in Britain because its Channel kept it safe from invasion for centuries at a time, without any need for the stifling presence of a standing army. For similar reasons, they transplanted readily to America and other lands, such as Australia and New Zealand, which enjoyed wide ocean barriers. In the case of Switzerland, virtually impenetrable mountains served in lieu of seas. And western Scandinavia is, of course, almost an island from the strategic standpoint. On the other hand, the democratic tradition rarely has prospered in countries such as Russia, China, and Germany, with great stretches of vulnerable land frontier.)

Consequently, it never occurred to the Bolsheviks to change in any fundamental way the normal protective apparatus of the Russian state. When Lenin spoke of seizing power, as he so often did, he apparently had in mind the police and military power above all else. This was, indeed, almost the only facet of the czarist state with which the revolutionists came in contact, and they naturally thought of power in police terms.

Even if the Communist founding fathers had wanted to abolish the political police system, they would not have dared. For they were faced immediately with counter-revolution, civil war, and invasion by the allied capitalist nations; and obviously they could survive only by the most desperate use of every weapon within reach. Inevitably, therefore, they took over the technique of the czar's *Okhrana*, and developed it into a cold, organized Terror, which Lenin once described as "the naked sword of the revolution." It was ironic (and rather sad) that the first boss of the new political police—then called the Cheka—should be Felix Dzerzhinsky, a gentle Polish-Lithuanian aristocrat, who sent his victims to their death with the most idealistic of motives. His successors have been more hard-boiled types.

As we noted in an earlier chapter, this police system has persisted—in accordance with the normal law of institutions—after the original reason for its existence disappeared. Today most Russians seem to accept it as a natural part of their environment, like the spring mud or the wind across the steppes. Yet they always feel its presence, for it is The Whip which helps to impose that universal discipline so essential to the Kremlin's ambitious plans.

Foreigners, too, are seldom permitted to forget the unceasing watchfulness of the police. It is true that visitors who spend only a week or two in the country sometimes report, with delighted surprise, that they were permitted to "go everywhere" without a police escort. This does not mean that they were not under surveillance, however, as older residents well know. The NKVD does not often need to use such crude methods as an escort or even a trailing plain-clothes man, because its agents are—almost literally—everywhere. After a little while you learn to recognize them without much trouble, and realize that you are seldom out of their sight.

Often these so-called secret police don't even make a pretense of secrecy. We encountered them at their most obvious in Kharkov, where a whole squad of detectives met the UNRRA delegation at the railway station, along with the deputy mayor and several minor city officials. The deputy mayor introduced everybody in the welcoming group except these NKVD men, and we gathered that the proper etiquette was to pretend that they were invisible. This was a little hard, because they rode in the same automobiles with us everywhere we went; the pistols in their hip holsters were plainly visible every time one of them leaned out to shout orders at a traffic cop or stooped to get through a car door. When we tried to inspect Kharkov's largest grocery store during its rush hour, six or eight additional gunsels suddenly appeared from nowhere to reinforce our regular guard. Facing outward, they formed a tight circle around us, so that we four Americans found ourselves standing in a conspicuously empty island in the middle of the crowded store. Later that evening, after a four-hour banquet, a detachment of these anonymous plain-clothes men accompanied us to our hotel rooms and took a quick look around the premises before we went to bed.

Eventually we discovered that these extraordinary precautions had resulted from a ludicrous misunderstanding. The Kharkov papers had printed an advance announcement of our visit, listing all of our names, including that of Marshall MacDuffie, the mission chief. The local officials had got the impression that "Marshall" was a title instead of a first name, and they had simply provided the protection which they considered appropriate for an eminent military commander.

As this incident indicates, the hovering presence of the NKVD is not altogether sinister. Every foreigner is regarded not only as a potential spy but also as a guest of the country. Consequently, the political police have a double duty: to make sure that you don't get into mischief, and to see that you are always safe and comfortable.

Often they turn out to be quite helpful. One evening, for example, I attended a concert with two other Americans. As we left the hall, we took our places in a long line of people waiting to get to the cloakroom. Suddenly a bald, grinning little man appeared out of the crowd, shouldered his way to the head of the line, and asked for our coats. He didn't have the checks, of course—they were still in our pockets—but the attendant handed over the coats without a word. Nor did anyone in the line protest at his breaking in, for they recognized Authority. The little man presented the proper coat to each of us, bowed, and disappeared into the crowd again.

An officer at the American embassy told me of a similar incident which occurred when he found himself stranded late one night in a small city some distance from Moscow. He had no hotel reservation, and he climbed aboard a streetcar near the railway station without much idea where it might take him or how he could find shelter for the night. A moment later a stranger standing at his elbow said, very politely: "If you are wondering how to get to the hotel, perhaps I can be of some help."

They left the streetcar together at the next stop. The stranger disappeared into the darkness for a few minutes and came back with an automobile. He directed the chauffeur to take them to the town's one hotel, which turned out to be—as usual—hopelessly overcrowded. Somebody was sleeping in every chair in the lobby, and at the desk the harassed night manager was trying ineffectually to cope with half a dozen angry late-comers. Several of them, evidently big men in the Party, were waving their credentials in the manager's face and bellowing that they must have rooms, while he kept repeating nervously: "But, comrades, there just aren't any."

The stranger didn't bellow. He merely whispered something into the manager's ear. The manager then vanished like a scared rabbit, leaving the Party big shots to fume alone. Ten minutes later the American was installed in a room from which some luckless guest obviously had just been expelled; the chambermaid was hastily putting fresh sheets on the bed.

Occasionally the NKVD will go to even more extreme lengths to make sure that foreigners are properly treated. Sir John Maynard in *The Russian Peasant*—one of the most illuminating studies of Soviet life—tells the story of a man who stole a foreigner's watch. "The law provides a penalty of three years' imprisonment for such a theft," Maynard notes. "But in this case the offender was shot. He was shot *for discrediting the USSR* in the eyes of foreigners."

While it takes such solicitous care of foreigners, the NKVD also makes sure that they do not contaminate any innocent Soviet citizen. In Moscow especially it is almost impossible to get on friendly terms with any Russians except those authorized to deal with strangers—foreign office and trade representatives, ballerinas, Intourist employees, cultural relations experts and such—who are sometimes known as "the reception committee." A number of Americans and Englishmen who had lived there for months told me that they had never been invited to a Russian home, nor had they been able to persuade any Russian to visit them. The American embassy is frankly quarantined; two NKVD men stand just outside the door, taking careful note of everyone who passes through. (One result is that the embassy never has to worry about thefts, even to the extent of locking up at night. "The penalty for burglary," an attaché explained, "is not nearly so high as the penalty for an unauthorized visit to our offices.") Paul Winterton in his *Report on Russia* summed up the situation in these words:

"The people whom one met in the street, or in the park, or around the town, were often friendly enough and ready to talk or listen as long as the conversation could be conducted inconspicuously—but only in the rarest cases did any closer acquaintance result. Most Russians, when they discovered you were a foreigner, shied away. . . . It wasn't that they felt sure they would get into trouble if they made friends—it was simply that they thought it would be better to take no risks."

It is only fair to note that as you get farther away from Moscow the invisible wall becomes less airtight. In some Ukrainian towns where no foreigners had penetrated for many years, we found that the people were actually eager to strike up friendships—presumably because the police had never had occasion to warn them against such behavior. Moreover, on trains and planes the Russian passengers usually did not hesitate to talk freely with us, unless some NKVD man happened to be present.

Shepherding visiting foreigners is perhaps the least of the NKVD's many duties. It has a number of routine functions, such as guarding the frontiers with a corps of specially uniformed Border Troops, who keep spies from slipping in and Soviet citizens from slipping out. The green-capped officers of this corps also serve as customs and passport inspectors. A separate corps of Internal Troops, with another distinctive uniform, guards public buildings, key industrial installations, and concentration camps. All local fire departments also are staffed by the NKVD.

Because the organization has enlisted a considerable proportion of the country's ablest men and has at its disposal a large and docile labor force of political prisoners, it often is given responsibility for carrying out important industrial projects. It has built a number of canals, railways, and war plants, for example, and is now in charge of developing atomic energy. (Or so, at least, most of the foreign diplomats in Moscow suppose; probably none of them has conclusive evidence, since no subject is more tightly wrapped in secrecy.)

Abroad, the NKVD has a widespread espionage network, operating independently of the various military and Party intelligence services. The Canadian Royal Commission on Russian espionage reported that the "organization in Canada is the result of a long preparation by trained and experienced men, who have come here for the express purpose of carrying on spying activities, and who have employed all the resources at their disposal, with or without corruption, to fulfill the tasks assigned to them." The Commission's 733-page report—the most reliable and carefully documented study ever published on Soviet espionage techniques—sets forth evidence that such spying started as early as 1924 and went on throughout the war, regardless of the fact that Canada was one of Russia's allies; that Canadian citizens were systematically bribed and seduced into treason; and that the NKVD setup in Canada was closely linked with similar organizations in the United States, Switzerland, England, and elsewhere. Incidentally, the Commission's investigation uncovered a curious list of NKVD code names. The Communist Party, for example, was always referred to in spy circles as "The Corporation"; "Gisel" stood for the Red Army intelligence service; "Metro" for the Soviet embassy; and "Lesovia" for Canada. A forger of passports was known as "a shoemaker" and NKVD agents (somewhat ominously) as "The Neighbors." New code words no doubt have been substituted since the publication of the report.

In the satellite countries of eastern Europe the NKVD

has helped the new governments to set up their own political police, such as Tito's impressively efficient OZNA in Yugoslavia, and has provided Russian experts to train the local recruits. It also has kept tabs on Soviet citizens in the occupied countries. In August 1946, for instance, a Mrs. Lena Herz-Krupenko was arrested by the American army in an UNRRA displaced persons' camp. She confessed that she was an NKVD agent and that she had got her job as chief physician in the camp in order to watch the Ukrainians who were there awaiting return to their homes.

By far the most important of the NKVD's duties, however, is the detection and punishment of "enemies of the people" within the Soviet Union. This term is mainly applied to political dissenters, but it also covers grafting factory managers, thieves caught stealing state property, workmen who break too many tools, and anyone who mutters too loudly about his pay, hours of labor, or the shortage of consumers' goods. Any action, in fact, which might discredit the government or hamper the fulfillment of the Five Year Plan is almost certain to bring down the fist of the political police.

Russian police methods have been so thoroughly described by Koestler, Kravchenko, Littlepage, Barmine, Gouzenko, and others with firsthand knowledge that it is hardly necessary to go into the details here. It is enough to note that their accounts and the few guarded comments I was able to pick up in Moscow and the Ukraine all agree on the basic techniques—constant espionage, concentrating especially on Party members and responsible officials; arrests in the dead of night; interminable questioning, coupled sometimes with more persuasive methods of extracting confessions; and finally the sentence to the execution cellar or concentration camp. From such a sentence there is no means of appeal.

Trials are granted to political offenders only on those rare occasions when the authorities decide that a public confession would provide a salutary lesson to the populace. (I have been unable to find any record of a political trial in which the accused did *not* confess, or in which the court failed to convict.) Even in ordinary criminal cases, the Russian concept of judicial procedure is quite different from our own. The Soviet court is never regarded as an independent tribunal, capable of protecting the citizen against illegal acts of the government. It is merely one of the instruments, along with the police and the Red Army, which the ruling class uses to impose its will. Thus directives of the Communist Party are enforced by the courts, whether or not they have ever been enacted into law by any formal legislative body. And the actions of the political police are, of course, never subject to any kind of judicial review.

One by-product of the NKVD's vigilance is a considerable supply of prison labor. I have no idea how large it may be. Published estimates range all the way from five to twenty million people, but none of them, so far as I can discover, is based on much beyond sheer speculation. Probably no one outside of the Kremlin has ever had access to reliable figures. Yet the total unquestionably is large, since vast construction projects—the Moscow-Volga canal, for example, and the double-tracking of the Trans-Siberian railway—have been attributed to prison labor in official Soviet reports.

The only prison camp I saw in the Ukraine was a small one near the Kharkov airport, so located that every traveler on the main highway from the airfield to the city has to pass within a few yards of it. It was simply a corral about one hundred yards square surrounded by a high barbed wire fence. At each corner stood a guard tower, manned by uniformed NKVD troops armed with tommy guns. Within the enclosure were two rows of brick and wood barracks which, from the outside, didn't look much worse than any other housing in the Ukraine. On both occasions when I drove past the camp about twenty or thirty people were lounging around the yard outside the barracks. Most of them appeared to be under thirty-five years old, and a few were in their teens. A number of the men were wearing fragments of Red Army uniforms. One boy was stretched out in the shade of a building reading a book, a few women were hanging bedding on a clothesline, and the rest just stood about in the limp attitudes of prisoners the world over. Nobody looked particularly undernourished and their clothing was no more ragged than that of most Russian peasants.

It is possible that this was not a labor camp but either a local jail or a staging area where prisoners are collected for shipment to the Arctic lumber camps and the new industrial centers beyond the Urals—the regions where most of them are said to be currently employed. If this conjecture is correct, it would account for both the idleness of the

Kharkov prisoners and for their relatively good appearance. In Washington I saw a Soviet documentary film of the building of the Moscow-Volga canal which gave a much grimmer impression of prison labor. It showed some thousands of workers who looked gaunt, tattered, and close to exhaustion. The published stories of those who claim detailed personal knowledge of labor camps—Kravchenko's *I Chose Freedom* is the most recent—also sketch a hair-raising picture of misery and cruel discipline. I have no way, of course, to judge the accuracy of such accounts.

My only other glimpse of civilian prisoners came during a trip from Kiev to Dnepropetrovsk. The train on which I was riding had a specially built prison car attached just behind the engine. During a long stopover at Znamenka I had a chance to stroll along the station platform and take a close-up look at this car. (My curiosity caused a good deal of anxiety to a minor Russian official named Miranov who happened to be traveling with me. He made almost frantic efforts to divert my attention to the scenery on the opposite side of the station.) The car's windows were barred with heavy iron latticework. Similar latticework doors shut off each of the ten compartments from the corridor, and solid steel doors were fitted at the ends of the car. Four uniformed guards lounged in the corridor, chatting through its barred windows with soldiers on the station platform. They paid no attention to me or my nervous companion, and very little to their prisoners.

There were about a score of these in sight—and again I was struck by their youthful appearance. One compart-

ment was crowded with women, all dressed in typical peasant clothes, who could hardly have been more than twenty
or twenty-five years old. Four of them clung to the
window bars and stared at the crowded station yard
with wooden, expressionless faces. Another compartment
housed a few men, and a third held a solitary woman. All
the others were empty, so far as I could see, although people may have been lying on the floor below my eye level.
In none of the compartments could I see any bunks or
fittings; they looked as bare as a steel cattle car. And for
all the interest displayed by the people around the station,
the car might have been hauling cattle.

On the basis of the scanty information available to out-
siders, it seems reasonable to draw four conclusions about
the Soviet political police system:

1. Its grip on every aspect of Russian life is so tight and
ruthless that no opposition movement is likely to make
much headway, even if discontent should become much
more widespread than it is at present.

2. It serves as an effective instrument of industrial, as
well as political, discipline, and if the current Five Year
Plan is completed on schedule, the NKVD can claim much
of the credit.

3. There is no prospect that the police system will be
relaxed, so long as the Soviet government feels that it must
hold down living standards in order to build up a great
defense industry for a coming war.

4. The NKVD's foreign espionage network probably

is the most efficient and far reaching in the world; in the words of the Canadian Investigating Commission, "in virtually all cases" its agents are "recruited from among cells or study groups . . . of the Communist Party" in each country where it operates.

CHAPTER
EIGHT

THE SMALL-TIME
SECRET AGENT

PAVEL PETROVICH PUROBAYEV WAS STRICTLY A small-time secret agent. No government in its right mind would have dreamed of using him to steal a radar blueprint or to worm state secrets out of a foreign diplomat. If he had ever been called upon to cope with a Mata Hari, he would have been disastrously likely to follow the methods of Harpo Marx rather than E. Phillips Oppenheim's. He carried out his assignments with the finesse of a grizzly bear —which, in fact, he strikingly resembled.

Yet he served the NKVD earnestly and well. He worshiped the Party and its Leader with granite fidelity, and I'm sure he would have died for them, if necessary, without wavering for an instant. He would have regretted it, however, for Purobayev was born to be a secret policeman and he enjoyed every minute of it.

When he was still a boy Purobayev had run away from his home village in the wheat country of central Russia to go to sea, and for the next twenty years he sailed all over the world on Russian, British, and Norwegian tramp freighters. In the course of this voyaging he had picked up a little English, firm views about the hard lot of the workingman, and a good deal of experience in dealing with foreigners. This rare combination of talents commended him to the Soviet political police, who recruited him into their plain-clothes department not long after the Revolution. The same accomplishments presumably led to his assignment to the UNRRA mission the day we arrived in Kiev.

Nominally Purobayev was the straw boss of the small local staff supplied to us by the Ukraine government. He looked after the office housekeeping, hired our automobile drivers, instructed the janitor's family in deportment, bought railway tickets, scrounged teacups and a kettle for our commissary, reserved theater seats, and carried our mail and cables to the post office. These duties fitted in nicely with his real job, which was to keep an eye on us and to make reports on all of our communications with UNRRA headquarters in Washington and London. He also was under orders to make sure that we enjoyed our stay in Russia and took home a happy impression of the country. All of this he did with an unbending resolution which led, in the beginning, to a few minor misunderstandings.

Soon after we had got settled in our office, for example, our interpreter decided to take a cable to the post office herself, just for the walk. Purobayev objected.

"You might get hurt," he explained.

Mary, ordinarily a placid little lady, pointed out with some temper that she had successfully dodged traffic in New York for thirty years and probably could do as well in Kiev.

"But maybe somebody will hit you with his fist," Purobayev said. "This is a free country and anyone can do
whatever he wants."

At that point Mary abandoned her English and the argument crackled on in Russian for some little time while
Purobayev's broad and leathery face got pink with embarrassment. In the end it dawned on her that all he really
wanted was to read the cable. We showed it to him on the
spot—it was merely an inquiry about an overdue shipment
of tractor parts—and from then on we made a translation
of every cable for Purobayev to turn over to his superiors.
This procedure greatly simplified his work, and it made no
difference to us, since there was nothing confidential in our
correspondence. (We also made a point of leaving our
desks and filing cabinets unlocked at night.) Purobayev
never again objected to our walking to the post office or
anywhere else. And of course nobody ever offered to hit
Mary or any of the rest of us on the street. People stared,
naturally, because our clothes marked us as foreigners, but
they were unfailingly polite.

Purobayev was grateful for our small gestures of co-
operation, and showed it. One Sunday he arranged a sight-
seeing trip to the old battlefield of Darnitsa, where the Red
Army had crossed the Dnieper in its surge toward Berlin.
When Mary suggested that she take along her camera,
Purobayev began to stutter and flop his stubby hands in
vague motions of distress.

"Well, if you don't want me to, just say so," Mary said,
"and I'll leave it at home."

"You don't know how much I would appreciate that,"

he answered. And all the rest of the afternoon he proved his gratitude by picking wild flowers and tearing great branches off pine trees to brighten up Mary's hotel room. He even lumbered into the underbrush, cap in hand, in an effort to catch a butterfly she had admired. It got away, but that bearlike figure, tiptoeing after a flicker of yellow among the raw shell holes and broken chunks of tank armor, made a memorable picture of contrition.

Only one other time did he ever interfere with our plans. That was at the opera one night shortly after our arrival in Kiev. While we were smoking in the lobby between acts, we met two sisters who worked as clerks in a government bureau with which we did business. They chatted with us for a few minutes, asking eager questions about America, and finally invited our whole party to tea in their apartment the following evening. Having said we would be delighted to visit a Ukrainian home, our interpreter warned that we might be dull guests since she alone spoke Russian and the girls understood no English.

"Oh, that'll be all right," one of them told Mary. "You can talk enough for everybody."

And she added, with a flash of typically Ukrainian humor: "We have a little brother who is a deaf-mute. He'll make good company for your other Americans."

Purobayev, who as usual had come to the theater with us, listened to all this in glum silence. When we asked him whether he could arrange for a car to take us to the tea party, he merely grunted. After the performance he didn't walk with us to our hotel as he ordinarily did but said an abrupt goodbye on the opera-house steps. Then he headed for the streetcar which the two sisters would have to take to their part of town.

Next day he did not show up at the office. We were unable to locate him by telephone. The girls did not call, as they had said they would, to give us directions to their home; nor did the car show up to take us to the party. We spent a lonely evening in the hotel, muttering about our private iron curtain.

Several days later, when we met one of the sisters at her office, she neither mentioned the incident nor renewed her invitation. Purobayev also avoided the subject; and so did we, since obviously he had only carried out his orders.

After a time, however, Purobayev (and his superiors) apparently decided that we were not bent on spying, spreading capitalist propaganda, or other clandestine shenanigans, because we eventually succeeded in visiting a number of Ukrainian homes and in using cameras quite freely. Even Purobayev himself finally thawed out enough to tell us something about his life.

It had not been an easy one. He had worked hard all his years at sea but had never saved much money—because, he said, "capitalist shipowners exploit poor seamen very bad." He thought a moment and then added in his hamstrung English: "Besides, I spend plenty money on whisky and women."

Buenos Aires, as he remembered it, was the best port for women.

"There was big roller-skating rink down by water front," he said. "As soon as ship docked all sailors used to go there and get good and drunk. Then we would put on roller skates and cotch girls."

Once, though, he had almost become a capitalist. At about the time of the Yukon gold rush, he had made fast friends with an Irish shipmate named Healy. They hoarded their pay through two long voyages, and when their vessel touched at Seattle both of them jumped ship. Their plan was to buy a prospector's outfit and head for Alaska to make their fortunes in the gold fields.

"We had nearly three thousand dollars for grubstake," Purobayev said, a little wistfully. "For two weeks we buy rifles, snowshoes, beans, shovels, and such things till we have just enough money left to pay fare to Alaska. All that time we didn't take one little drink.

"The night before we are suppose to leave for Nome, I come back to hotel and find Healy sitting on our bed in his undershirt with big bottle of whisky. He also has big redheaded girl sitting on his lap. I think what the hell maybe I better have a little drink myself before we start for all that deep snow. So pretty soon bottle was empty and I go out for some more whisky. On my way back I meet a girl, too. Very nice.

"For three days we have fine farewell party. Then all our passage money was gone, so we don't go to Alaska after all. Healy and me sell our rifles and snowshoes and have another little party. Then we ship out on freighter with a cargo of wheat for Peru."

He was full of other pre-Revolutionary tales—about the Crimean bank clerk who "wore a little curling machine on his face every night" in hopes of making his mustache turn up at the ends like Kaiser Wilhelm's, and about the week-old baby girl someone had left in Purobayev's railway compartment while he was sleeping off a hangover.

About his more recent life under the Soviets, however, he was stubbornly reticent. He told me only that he had spent the war in a rear echelon of the Red Army, that he had won five medals, and that he had learned the trick of sleeping in the snow in sub-zero weather without freezing to death.

"You must take turns with another soldier," he said. "After you sleep for three minutes—no more—he must wake you up. Then you run around in circle, stomping feet hard, for three minutes while he sleeps. If you let him sleep too long, he never wake up."

The Germans' failure to learn this technique, Purobayev thought, was largely responsible for their heavy losses in the winter campaigns.

"If they know how to sleep better, maybe they win war, who knows?"

His two sons had been killed in the war, and his wife—a surgeon—had developed a bad heart from overwork. Puro-bayev himself suffered from a heart complaint which had forced him to give up most of the pleasures of his youth, including vodka. He was still as strong as a Brahmany bull —I've seen him heave a jeep out of axle-deep mud single-handed—but he often spoke of himself as "a worn-out old man."

That didn't keep him from serving us just as energeti-cally as he did the NKVD. He was a first-class operator, with a profound knowledge of Soviet red tape and how to get around it, plus an old soldier's knack for scrounging anything he couldn't get through official channels. He kept us well supplied with coal and kindling, for instance, when fuel was almost unobtainable in Kiev, and as a result, our office was about the warmest place in the city throughout the long, cold spring. Moreover, Purobayev kept the lesser members of our Ukrainian staff up to a high pitch of discipline.

Especially Yakov S. Brovkin and his family. They were peasants whom Purobayev had hired as caretakers for the seven-room house at 9 Pavlovskaya Street, which had been converted into offices for the UNRRA mission. Mr. and Mrs. Brovkin and their three daughters lived in two small basement rooms.

Papa Brovkin, who often managed to get comfortably primed with vodka by ten in the morning, did nothing but tend the small garden. His wife dusted, swept out, and waxed the office floors; whenever the gloss fell short of Purobayev's standards, he told her off with a thunderous rumble of Russian adjectives. Galya, the sixteen-year-old daughter, kept the keys, emptied the wastebaskets, and stoked the tile stove which heated our baths. (We frequently had to bathe at the office, since our hotel seldom managed to produce hot water more than once a week.)

Under Purobayev's stern instruction, the entire Brovkin family usually turned up at the front door to greet us with low bows when we arrived for work in the mornings. Galya once informed us, in a confidential moment, that she had been told to "love and respect all of the UNRRA

Americans." Consequently, she changed into her Sunday clothes every time she came upstairs to bring us a pot of tea or to announce that a bath was ready. Even Holya, the six-year-old, treated us with grave deference, and got over her shyness only after we adopted her as a sort of office mascot.

A question of discipline finally resulted in the Brovkins' leaving us. One chilly spring morning we heard strange squeals in the back yard, and on investigation found that Papa Brovkin had bought a skinny yellow pig which he had penned up in a corner of the garden. He explained that his was a farm family which wouldn't feel at home unless they could fatten a pig or two; and besides, they needed the meat to piece out their rations.

That was all right with us—the pig seemed as clean and quiet as one could reasonably expect—but it wasn't all right with Purobayev. He made an outraged speech, pointing out that the ambassadorial dignity of the UNRRA mission would be undermined for good if a hog grew up in our back yard. Moreover, Purobayev objected to the janitor's vodka-tippling, and to his lack of vigilance in guarding our supplies in the basement storeroom.

The upshot was that the pig went to the country, and the Brovkins along with it. After the customary two weeks' notice, they piled their belongings on a two-wheeled cart, said tearful farewells to all of us, and headed for their native village about twenty miles away. A suitable replacement apparently was hard to find, because we had to do without janitor service for some time after.

There were a few other minor mishaps which Purobayev

couldn't avert for all his skill and thoroughness. For instance, the American embassy in Moscow once had to relay an inquiry from Mary's husband in New York; he hadn't heard from her in more than a month and wanted to know what had happened. We then discovered that three personal cables which Mary had sent to him had not been dispatched. Some girl clerk in the Kiev post office had simply decided that they were not important and had stuffed them into the "Permanently Deferred" file.

Mary took her indignation out on Purobayev, who, she said, never should have permitted such a thing to happen. He listened to her tongue-lashing for twenty minutes, looking thoroughly miserable, and then apologized on behalf of himself, the post office, the Ministry of Communications, and the Ukrainian government.

"Those girls in the cable section are just stupid working people," he said sorrowfully. "How can we ever teach them to do their job right?"

On the whole, however, Purobayev proved an invaluable fellow, both because of his own virtues and his connection with the secret police. This sometimes produced results when nothing else would. In a pinch it could even give him authority above that of a major general—as it did the night our train broke down.

On that occasion I woke up about midnight to find that our car had been shunted onto a siding at some half-ruined station on the empty prairie a hundred miles or more north of Dnepropetrovsk. A porter stuck his head into the compartment which I shared with two other Americans and a

Russian girl who was serving as our interpreter on that trip. He told us to dress fast and get out of the car. He also removed the only electric-light bulb in the compartment. All the bulbs in the car were his personal responsibility, he said, and if he didn't collect them before the passengers got out, they would surely be stolen.

We dressed in the dark as best we could, and I went to find Purobayev, who was sharing a neighboring compartment with three soldiers. He was struggling into the old Red Army uniform which was evidently the only suit of clothes he owned. (I never saw him wear anything else, at any rate. Like many another Russian soldier, Purobayev had reconverted to civilian status merely by removing his epaulets and other official insignia.) I held a pocket lighter for him while he wrapped his feet in the strips of white cloth—probably from a worn-out bedsheet—which served him in lieu of socks. He pulled on his knee-length black leather boots, adjusted a celluloid collar under the neck of his tunic, and combed his long, sandy hair with calm deliberation. Then we sallied out to see what the trouble was.

Our car, we discovered, had developed a hotbox, and the train crew had sidetracked it to await repair by the local maintenance men next day. This meant that the passengers would have to sit around in the rubble of that forlorn station for twenty-four hours. There was no hotel within many miles, and the rest of the train was too crowded to accommodate us. It was, in fact, on the point of pulling away without us at that very moment.

The other people in our car seemed to accept their predicament with Slavic resignation. All of them—including a major general, three colonels, and a couple of middling-important bureaucrats—listened to the porter's orders without protest and began to strap up their luggage.

But not Purobayev. He announced quietly that we could all go back to bed. The car would be repaired immediately, he said, and the train would wait for us. He then waddled off, with his rolling sailor's gait, to interview the engineer and station master.

He must have showed them his NKVD credentials and made some pointed remarks about Siberia, for things began to happen fast. Within five minutes a repair crew came running down the track toward our car as if pursued by devils. They were the only workmen I saw during my whole stay in Russia who really hurried. Three of them held torches, made of rags dipped in kerosene, while the others fell to with wrenches and sledge hammers. Meanwhile, the engineer backed his train onto our siding and prepared to recouple. The porter brought back the light bulbs. The station master appeared, hat in hand, and apologized to everybody in sight. One of the colonels produced a bottle of vodka and suggested that we all have a nightcap before turning in again. Before the bottle was empty, the burned-out bearing had been replaced and we were on our way again.

Next morning the general tendered his formal thanks to our party "for using your diplomatic influence to avoid an uncomfortable delay for all the comrades in this car." Purobayev looked smug and said nothing.

The most disagreeable part of Purobayev's job was his responsibility to see that we enjoyed ourselves. He bought tickets for the opera, concerts, and ballet—which were virtually the only entertainments Kiev afforded—as often as he could persuade us to attend. What's more, he went along with us "to see that everything goes all right," even though classical music was by no means his dish. Ballet was not so bad, because Purobayev still had a sharp eye for a well-built wench, but at the opera he suffered the deepest torments of boredom. He would sit at the back of our box, wriggling on a spindly chair which was not half big enough for his plump bottom, his eyes glazed and his hands clasped over his paunch. From time to time he would doze off, only to jerk awake whenever the soprano hit a high note.

After the performance of *Othello*, an opera that he found even duller than most, he asked me as we walked home whether the Salvation Army bands still played along the Embarcadero in San Francisco. I told him that, so far as I knew, they did.

"I often heard them there when I was a sailor," he said. "Now that was good, honest music."

His idea of real fun was hunting and fishing, and he coaxed us endlessly to spend an afternoon with him in the woods or along the banks of the Dnieper. We never had time for that, but he did lure us into a number of evening picnics. The most catastrophic of these occurred the night before I left Kiev to return to the United States.

He came into the office about three o'clock that afternoon, while I was rushing frantically to finish off countless odds and ends of work. He shook hands rather formally, as was his custom, put an ingratiating grin on his face, and sat down in the middle of the papers spread all over my desk. It struck me then that he looked precisely like The Good Soldier Schweik.

"We have very fine farewell picnic tonight," he announced.

That was out of the question, I told him. I had to work late, pack, and catch a few hours' sleep before the plane left at 6 A.M.

"But it will be short picnic," he said. "Maybe only two hours. If you don't come, all your friends in Kiev will feel very bad. In Ukraine it is custom to have small fraternal picnic whenever friend goes away."

I finally gave in, of course, as I nearly always did when the old wheedler really settled down to work on me.

We set out just before sundown in a caravan of jeeps, army trucks, and battered touring cars. They carried all the Americans from our office, plus some twenty Ukrainians from the government bureaus with which we worked most closely. They also carried an astonishing cargo of vodka, hard-boiled eggs, pickled herring, black bread, raw onions, smoked salmon, cheese, bloodwurst, fried fish, and beer. It looked like enough to feed a regiment of the Red Army for a month.

Purobayev supervised the deployment of these victuals on a grassy knoll above the Dnieper, perhaps ten miles south of the city. He opened the bottles himself and started pouring vodka into eight-ounce water tumblers, which he filled clear to the brim. Then he proposed a toast to my safe flight home.

Now, putting away eight ounces of vodka at a single gulp struck me as a suicidal business, but there was no way to avoid it without insulting everybody in the crowd. The best I could do was to plead for a moment's delay, while I choked down a big hunk of black bread and cheese in hopes that it would provide a kind of protective foundation. Everybody drank, bottoms up—including Purobayev with his bad heart. Then he filled up the glasses again.

I managed to spill most of my second drink, even though we were toasting Generalissimo Stalin, The Peerless Leader, and after that I shifted to beer. Most of the Russians stuck to vodka, pausing between toasts only long enough to eat a few pounds of raw onions and pickled herring. By the time the moon came up all the food was gone, empty bottles were strewn all over the hillside, and a couple of romantic Ukrainian statisticians were chasing our prettiest American stenographer through the underbrush.

It was nearly midnight before I could persuade Purobayev to take me back to the hotel to begin my packing. We found a jeep driver who seemed to be still capable of hanging on to a steering wheel and started weaving back toward Kiev over one of the roughest cobblestone roads ever laid by human hands. Then, just before we reached the ramshackle suburbs of the city, Purobayev broke the bad news. We couldn't go to the hotel yet, he said, because the cleaning shop which was working on my best suit had forgotten to return it. At that hour of night and in our somewhat disorganized condition, I couldn't see much hope of finding it, but we had to try, since I could hardly afford to leave Russia without it.

Because the jeep driver had trouble focusing his eyes on the street signs, it took us some time to locate the cleaning shop. It was closed, naturally; but after beating on the doors of half a dozen neighboring houses we finally aroused an old woman who could tell us the name of the manager.

It was Fremkin, and she thought he lived on the other side of town.

On our way there we got lost in the maze of dark, deserted streets, and wandered for half an hour before we came across a policeman. He thought he ought to arrest us for roaming around drunk at such an unseemly hour—probably in a stolen jeep—but Purobayev talked him out of that. Eventually the cop gave us directions to the street where Fremkin was supposed to live.

We pounded on every door in the block without getting any response. Then the three of us stood in the middle of the street and shouted "Fremkin" in chorus. At last a light went on in a second-floor apartment, and a man stuck his head out the window.

"I'm Fremkin," he said. "What do you want?"

Purobayev explained, adding that the recovery of my suit was a matter of the utmost diplomatic urgency.

"As unlikely a story as I ever heard," Fremkin commented. "Personally, I think you are robbers with a clever scheme to loot my shop. And it won't work."

After considerable negotiation, he agreed to drop a string down from his window. I tied onto it my passport and ticket for the morning's plane, and he pulled them up for examination. That convinced him. He dressed, came downstairs, and accompanied us to the shop, where we located the suit, still damp with cleaning fluid, in a heap of officers' uniforms. When we took Fremkin back to his apartment, he shook hands with all of us and made me promise to send him a bulletin on modern cleaning methods from the United States.

Purobayev and I finally got to the hotel to find that the survivors of the picnic had gathered in my room to continue the party. They sang Cossack ballads for me while I packed, pausing now and then to urge me to join them in one last fraternal toast. Under these circumstances, sleep was impracticable. It was all I could do to get my bag strapped shut in time to leave for the airport at 5 A.M.

My small-time secret agent came along to say goodbye. As he heaved my luggage into the plane, he observed with a happy grin that he had never attended a more successful picnic.

"You must understand that Russians are very friendly people," he said. "They need to have such picnic to wish you a soft road home."

CHAPTER
NINE

WHAT MAKES THE
WORKING CLASS WORK

I<small>F YOU WANT TO SEE THE</small> C<small>OMMUNIST TECHNIQUE</small> of The Cookie and The Whip in its fullest blossom, the place to look is in the factories. Since the rapid development of industry comes first in all the Kremlin's plans, the Party has assigned some of its best brains to devise schemes for extracting the last possible ounce of labor from every factory worker.

The most effective scheme they have produced so far is the piecework system. It has been introduced wherever technically feasible, so that now the typical Russian laborer does not draw a fixed weekly wage but gets paid according to the number of shoes or tank parts or yards of cloth he turns out.

This arrangement automatically provides both a goad and a lure. It has many variations, but usually each worker is assigned a "norm" or minimum number of pieces which he is supposed to produce every day. If his output falls much below this figure, he is sure to go hungry, and he is likely to be fired. If he produces more than his "norm," on the other hand, he gets a bonus for every extra piece he makes. In many factories the bonus increases on a rising scale—one ruble for the first ten units above the "norm," two rubles for the next ten, and so on. Under the new Five Year Plan these incentive pay schemes will be expanded, so that a really diligent and clever workman can make ten or twelve times as much money as his more sluggish comrades.

Outside of Russia, trade unionists generally are opposed to the piecework system, and as a result it has been abandoned in a good part of British and American industry. In the capitalist countries nobody has fought it more bitterly than the Communists. They are always ready to explain, however, that they are not guilty of any real inconsistency. I have heard Vassily Kuznetzov, boss of all the Soviet trade unions, argue brilliantly that piecework is a vicious thing in the Western nations because predatory capitalists use it to exploit their workers, but that it is a good thing in the USSR because all industry there is owned by the workers themselves, and every speed-up therefore redounds to their own benefit. The duller members of the working class, even in Russia, sometimes have a little trouble in grasping this point.

There is another difficulty with piecework methods which holds just as true in the USSR as it does elsewhere: it is likely to encourage a high quantity of production at the cost of low quality. The result is plain in nearly all the brick walls, for example, which have been laid in Russia within the last twenty years. They show unmistakable evidence that the bricks were slapped together at top speed, with little attention to standards of masonry. Typically, the courses are uneven and some joints lack mortar altogether, while big lumps of surplus cement protrude from others.

Presumably such defects might be avoided, even under the piecework system, by close supervision and ingrained traditions of craftsmanship. These are just the two things, however, which Soviet industry most grievously lacks— · through no fault of its own. It has simply not had time to train the hundreds of thousands of supervisors and foremen it needs; and the great majority of its laborers are former peasants, who have barely been able to learn their trade, much less the refinements of craftsmanship. (Many of them, indeed, have not yet mastered the theory of lubrication. Machinery is damaged every day because somebody forgot to oil it, and I have seen expensive machine tools sitting in railway cars, open to the weather, without a trace of grease or cosmolene to protect them.) These handicaps, I believe, account for most of the complaints of poor quality—especially in consumers' goods—which show up in the self-criticism columns of the Soviet press. They may be overcome in time, for they do not appear to be inherent in the Communist scheme of production.

In addition to the piecework system, a considerable assortment of other rewards and punishments is used to spur on the Soviet worker. His most widely advertised blessing is, of course, security: he never has to worry about mass unemployment, and if he should be crippled in an industrial accident he can be sure that he and his family would be cared for by the state. Moreover, if he makes an exceptionally good record, he may be permitted to spend an occasional vacation at one of the rest homes in the Caucasus mountains or on the Crimean coast. If he stifles the impulse —endemic among Russians—to flit from one job to another, he can eventually qualify for a discount on all goods sold in the luxury stores; and an unusual spurt of production may earn him a couple of tickets to the theater. (It is noteworthy that the theaters are among the first buildings being restored in war-damaged Ukrainian cities. The Parks of Culture and Rest—Soviet versions of Coney Island— also are high on the priority list. One mayor told me that he had no hopes of providing enough living space, clothes, or food to satisfy his people for a long time to come, and therefore it was all the more necessary to give them as many amusements as possible.) Finally, outstanding workers are encouraged by a liberal buttering of glory and public acclaim; they get the kind of newspaper publicity which in America is reserved for movie stars and the glamor girls of café society.

On the other hand, the Russian workingman cannot hope to better himself very much by trade union action. It is not true that strikes are legally forbidden in the USSR —they aren't mentioned in the judicial code. A few of them actually have occurred since the end of the war, but they have little chance of accomplishing anything. They can't win higher wages, because the total amount of each industry's payroll is rigidly fixed in the over-all Plan; management couldn't grant a raise even if it wanted to. Furthermore, Soviet trade unions just aren't set up for collective bargaining. They collect no strike funds and have no real negotiating committees. The rare strikes which do break out are wildcats, called in defiance of the union. The rank-and-file workers who lead them are virtually certain to end up in a concentration camp—technically not for striking but for "sabotage" and "spreading unrest."

For the purpose of trade unions in the USSR is almost the exact opposite of what it is in the Western world. They are not designed to fight for higher pay but rather to prod, educate, and exhort their members into higher production. Their prime duty is not to represent the workers in dealings with the boss but to help The Boss—that is, the Politburo—in handling its labor problems. They are simply one of the many arms of the Kremlin. Their officers are elected under Party direction, and their first responsibility is to carry out the Party's will. If "industrial democracy" means participation by the ordinary workingman in determining industrial policy, then there clearly is far less of it in Russia than in America. Through his unions and political pressure, the American worker exercises an influence on management which his Soviet counterpart could never dream of.

The Soviet unions have been so thoroughly integrated into the machinery of the state that they carry out many functions which in the United States are performed by government agencies—notably the Social Security Board, state and federal employment services, and the bureaus which enforce safety and sanitary regulations. From the standpoint of discipline, this arrangement offers many advantages. If a worker shows signs of becoming "un-cooperative," for example, he may encounter some difficulty in collecting the social insurance or workman's compensation payments due him. Or if he turns out to be a trouble-maker in one plant, he is not likely to be able to get an equally good job elsewhere, for his file will follow wherever he goes, through the intricate channels of the Joint Trade Union Congress.

Naturally the unions have had to build up a considerable bureaucracy to handle their clerkly functions—keeping books on social insurance alone requires a small army of accountants—so it is hardly surprising that their officials occasionally acquire bureaucratic habits. *Trud*, the national trade union newspaper, recently started a vigorous campaign against "the soulless, formal bureaucratic attitude toward complaints and requests," which some officials have developed, and urged a return to "the Bolshevik teaching of contact with the masses." In particular, it denounced union officers in the Don Basin who had done nothing to improve "intolerable . . . labor and living conditions" and had got their books so muddled that labor crews "have not been paid for the last six months." Among the unfortunate conditions it reported were "dirty and uncomfortable" workers' hostels, people sleeping in corridors and tents "without the elementary amenities," and the loss of work time because laborers were sent to their jobs without tools or materials.

All this does not mean that the unions are of no benefit to the average Russian workingman. The cases cited by *Trud* probably were exceptional, and no doubt the Party is doing all it can to remedy them. Most union officers seem to be conscientious men who not only work hard at their main job of encouraging production but also perform many minor services for their members. They hear complaints about such things as dirty washrooms and bad cooking in the plant restaurant, and call them to the attention of the management. On occasion they even achieve the dismissal of unpopular factory directors. They also listen for rumblings of deeper discontent, and warn the Party bosses when a really far-reaching change in policy—an increase in the supply of consumers' goods, for example—seems necessary to cope with it.

Perhaps most important of all, the unions serve as a kind of giant sausage machine geared to convert raw, uncivilized peasants into acceptable members of a modern, urban society. To this end, they conduct "cultural-educational activities" in the clubrooms attached to nearly every factory. Here the new recruit from the village gets housebroken. Under the union's guidance he learns many things—how to behave at a dance, the theory of Leninism, chess, personal hygiene, and algebra. He may be invited to play in the club orchestra or to run the movie projector on Saturday nights. He can go to technical lectures which will help prepare him for a better job, or read up on international politics in the club library. If he is ambitious, he can begin his apprenticeship for the Communist Party. And, inevitably, he hears a great many speeches about how important it is for everybody to work a little harder in order to complete the Five Year Plan on schedule.

Yet many Soviet workers seem to have developed a certain immunity to such exhortations. In Zaporozhe a big red-and-white billboard had been erected in the courtyard of a bombed-out hospital where a repair gang was at work. Its slogan read: "Work harder today than you did yesterday. Accomplish more tomorrow than you do today."

When I walked into the courtyard, in the company of the mayor and the city's chief construction engineer, seven laborers were stretched out comfortably in the shade of this signboard. They were watching an eighth workman who was leisurely mixing a tub of concrete. They observed us with casual interest, but nobody felt impelled to spring into action just because the boss had showed up; nor did the mayor and the engineer appear to think there was anything unusual about the scene.

The incident was, at bottom, just one more symptom of the weariness and the let-down in morale which are natural after-effects of the Russians' tremendous war effort. It also illustrated the lack of foremen, which is one of the most crippling weaknesses in the Soviet economy. The effects of this shortage, at its worst, I saw at Dneprostroy, where thirteen thousand laborers were rebuilding the great dam across the Dnieper river.

The job was in charge of an engineer named Feodor Loginov, a six-foot bull-chested blond who looked like a Minnesota Swede. He had worked under Hugh Cooper, the American engineer who originally built the dam in the early thirties. So had his two chief assistants, both of whom had studied in the United States. These three are probably the best dam men in the USSR; they would be considered good in any country.

When they moved in, on the heels of the retreating Reichswehr, they found that the Germans had touched off six hundred tons of explosive under the turbines, generators, and the dam itself. Nothing much was left except a tangle of girders and shattered concrete in the middle of the Dnieper rapids. To clean up this mess, they could call on the government for a few inexperienced technicians just out of engineering college. All other labor had to be recruited locally. Since nearly every able-bodied man was in the Red Army, this meant hiring women—mostly farm girls who had never seen any tool more complicated than a hoe. After the fall of Berlin some men were assigned to the project, but when I was there in the spring of 1946 forty per cent of the construction gangs still were women. Even the guards at the equipment dumps were barefoot girls, armed with rifles and bayonets; one of them had her braids tied up in a blue hair ribbon.

The scene at the construction site would have given any American engineer a permanent case of shudders. Thousands of women were scrambling over the rubble heaps and the half-finished face of the dam with no more apparent direction than a hill of ants. A typical workwoman was one old grandmother with gnarled hands and a peasant shawl over her head whom I watched for about twenty minutes. She shuffled up to a pile of lumber, shouldered a ten-foot plank, and started out on the scaffolding which stretched across the downriver side of the dam. She picked her way carefully, because the flooring consisted of loose, curved metal plates salvaged from the wrecked generators.

If she had stepped too close to the edge of one of them, it would have tilted her into the frothing rapids some thirty feet below.

Every few yards she stopped to ask whether anybody could use her plank. Some of the workmen simply ignored her. Others laid down their tools and discussed the problem at length. One group of female carpenters even tried, without success, to fit it into the concrete form they were hammering together. At one point she had to dodge a stream of water as thick as a man's arm which was spurting through a crevice in the dam. (Somebody, Loginov explained later, had evidently miscalculated the shrinkage of setting concrete; the crevice wasn't really dangerous, and could be patched up at leisure.) In the end the old woman got discouraged and left her plank lying on the edge of the scaffold; if anybody ever needed a board of that particular size, presumably he would find it there sooner or later.

Similar odds and ends of lumber, cable, and forgotten tools were lying all over the place, and much of the equipment—such as American-made jackhammers and air compressors—was being used by people who obviously didn't know how to handle it. (One length of air hose blew up almost under my feet, and it was ten minutes before anybody discovered how to shut off the pressure.)

Yet the dam was going up. The first of the new turbine-and-generator aggregates was scheduled to go into operation early in 1947; it will turn out ten thousand more kilowatts of power than the sixty-two-thousand-kilowatt aggregate that it is replacing.

It is a mistake—to which Americans are peculiarly vulnerable—to assume that the Russians can't get things done because of their obvious shortages of technicians, straw bosses, and skilled labor. Anyone who has traveled in the USSR can tell plenty of stories about the ineptness and puttering tempo of Russian laborers. I saw many such examples myself—a seventeen-year-old girl carrying bricks in her arms because nobody had shown her how to use a hod; the electrician who left a snarl of loose wiring dangling from the wall like a handful of spaghetti; the eight men who took half a day to move a few hundred pounds of office supplies from a delivery truck into our office storeroom. (This particular crew restacked each box three or four times, pausing frequently for excited debate about what ought to go where. They also took a good deal of time off for simple gossip—as do most Russians. This habit is common to most peasant peoples, but in the Soviet Union it probably gets an extra stimulus from the austere character of the press, which carries virtually no items about such homely happenings as births, funerals, marriages, and crime. Consequently, such news has to travel by the grapevine, which operates with astonishing speed and coverage.)

What we are likely to forget is that the Soviet economy is uniquely designed to make up for these shortcomings by means of centralized planning. The Russians readily admit that their output per man hour is low, but they usually manage to offset it (as they are at Dneprostroy) by pouring in almost unlimited amounts of unskilled manpower, under a few top-flight managers.

This, of course, means concentrating labor on the few

things the Kremlin considers important, particularly the rebuilding of heavy industry. That in turn means a continuing shortage of consumers' goods, a long delay in housing, a degree of regimentation which people less docile than the Russians might find intolerable. The Communists, however, regard it as one of the great virtues of their system that the government need not be diverted by the public's weak and shortsighted cravings for the good things of life.

Americans also are likely to be misled by the fact that a Russian factory or construction job generally looks untidy. William L. White, for example, in his *Report on the Russians,* told about his visit to an aircraft factory that was "poorly lit and unbelievably dirty. . . . The floors throughout are uneven with holes in the concrete. Piles of metal shavings are everywhere." Then he quoted Eric Johnston, the American manufacturer who accompanied him, as saying:

"Back in the States the best rough test I know of the efficiency of any factory is its cleanliness. Any dirty shop is sure to be an inefficient one."

In Russia that test is not necessarily reliable. Part of the sloppiness in Soviet factories is due to the necessity of manning them largely with farm hands, at best only a few years away from the barnyard, who have not yet had a chance to absorb the instinctive disciplines of industry. Another reason, however, is that Russians just don't give a damn about the things they consider nonessential. They can't afford to waste time or scarce materials on what seems to them mere spit-and-polish. One Russian general, for instance, told me he could never understand why Americans bothered to machine the outside of cannon barrels. The Red Army doesn't care how rough the outer metal of its gun barrels may be, but the inner surface and riflings are tooled just as accurately as American ordnance.

Safety devices sometimes come under the heading of unnecessary frills. Most of the flying I did inside Russia was in Soviet-built aircraft patterned after the Douglas DC-3, without, as one pilot put it, "a lot of fancy work." That means that the planes are made without wing flaps, deicers, safety belts, or "No Smoking" signs. (Passengers habitually light up as they climb aboard, and keep right on smoking through the final landing. What's more, they sometimes stretch out in the shadow of the wing during stopovers and puff comfortably on their cigarettes while the gas truck is pumping fuel into the tanks just over their heads.) The plane interiors usually were free of both upholstery and paint, and they were seldom clean. The lavatories, in particular, seemed to be chronically ignored by the ground crews, and what little plumbing there was rarely worked.

Neither passengers nor baggage was ever weighed on any flight I made in Russia, apparently on the sound enough theory that a DC-3 will lift anything you can put into it. (The ATC pilots I knew in India during the war held much the same notion.) I remember, with shudders, one trip on which the entire space between the bucket seats running along either side of the plane was stacked high with crates of heavy machinery. Some twenty passengers clambered on top of these boxes or hunched themselves up on the aluminum seats. When the pilot climbed aboard, last of all, he shook his head dubiously.

"Looks too heavy," he said. "Somebody better get off."
Nobody moved.

"This is a short field," he added, "and I don't think I can lift her with this load."

Still nobody moved. The pilot—a wiry, hard-bitten youngster wearing a ragged sweater and a cloth cap—finally shrugged.

"All right," he said. "We'll try it. Move as far up front as you can, and I'll try to get the tail up."

We crowded to the head of the compartment. The pilot gunned his motors—Russian fliers seldom bother with a warm-up—and rolled the plane sluggishly down the runway. It was snowing, and as I peered out the window I couldn't see the fence that marked the end of the field. At last the plane tilted sharply upward—and at almost the same instant I saw the fence just below us. We must have cleared it only by inches because I could see the barbs on the wire quite distinctly. When one of the passengers, a bald-headed colonel, broke out a bottle of vodka a few minutes later, I didn't say no.

On this flight the cargo, as usual, was not lashed down. When we hit a patch of rough weather, the more nervous passengers (including myself) leaned forward and grabbed hold of the nearest crates to keep them from jumping in our laps. It was rough most of the time, too, because Soviet pilots prefer to fly at from five hundred to fifteen hundred feet. Most of their navigation apparently is done by contact, and they like to keep the landmarks within easy view.

Nevertheless, I never saw a plane accident in Russia or even heard an engine miss a beat. The working parts of all aircraft seemed to be competently maintained, and the pilots clearly knew their business. Some of them had an annoying habit of handling a transport like a fighter plane, yanking it into tight climbing banks at fifty feet above the ground, but they also could put it down on a rolling cow pasture or field covered with eight inches of snow as gently as a settling leaf.

During a long wait between planes at the Minsk airport, a young air-line officer explained to me the Soviet theory of doing without de-icers and similar gadgets.

"Sure we have a few more crack-ups," he said. "Maybe ten per cent more than if we had all those safety devices. But by leaving them off, we can build fifteen or twenty per cent more planes a year. So we are still five or ten per cent ahead."

It was characteristic that human life didn't enter into this calculation. This wasn't callousness. It was simply a habit, ingrained for centuries, of thinking of life in Asiatic rather than Western terms. The Russians' views on neatness also are somewhat Oriental; but it would be wrong to jump to the conclusion that they are therefore hopeless incompetents.

It should be noted, too, that the better Soviet workers often make up for their lack of skill and methodical habits —in part at least—by enthusiasm. True enough, there are thousands whose morale is low and who look on their work as nothing more than irksome drudgery. But there are others who take a shining pride in their jobs and in their factories, and who earnestly believe that they are working to build an ideal Communist world. This spirit sometimes enables them to tackle undertakings which laborers in other countries might well consider impossible.

The Mikoyan canning factory, just outside Kiev, was half destroyed by the Germans and looted of all its modern equipment. (Most of the machinery was sent by train to Kassel, where it was destroyed soon after arrival in an American air raid on the freight yard.) Any sensible manager would have concluded that the plant could not possibly get back into production until the buildings were reconstructed and new machinery brought in. Yet in the spring of 1946 it was turning out 250,000 cans and jars of food a month, or about a quarter of its prewar rate.

There was no glass for the shattered windows, so the factory employees filled up the empty frames with defective glass jars, cemented together to form a passable substitute for glass brick. Hand-operated machinery, obsolete for fifty years, was reclaimed from a junk yard. An old bearing off a railway car was converted into a makeshift device for stamping flanges on can lids. Wooden pipes were substituted for the stainless steel the Nazis had stolen. None of this was very efficient—but it worked.

Moreover, the employees were proud to the point of cockiness over what they had accomplished. They insisted on their foreign visitors sampling every variety of fruit and pickles which the factory put up—and all were tasty. In their spare time, the workers had rebuilt an attractive clubroom and a plant dining hall, and they were at work on a project to repair beds, salvaged from burned-out homes, for use in a neighboring hospital. These particular people offered an apt illustration of what a Hearst correspondent —no defender of Communism—once concluded about another group of Soviet workingmen:

"You would think they owned the country. Maybe they do, and maybe they don't; but they think so, and I have never seen the slave who thought he was the boss."

Some of the more choleric critics of the Soviet Union speak frequently of its "slave labor," as if all Russians worked under conditions of bondage. This, of course, is not true. The majority of Soviet citizens are free to choose their own jobs, quit when they please, and hunt work in other parts of the country if the grass looks greener there. Many of them, in fact, shift from job to job so restlessly that labor turnover is a constant worry to the government. I frequently saw "Help Wanted" advertisements, and talked to lots of train passengers who were bound for some distant city where they hoped to find better pay, housing, or food supplies.

It is true, however, that Russia uses more forced labor than any other country. It falls into five separate classes, each under a different degree of compulsion. The total unquestionably runs well into the millions.

The group which is best off consists of Communist Party members and the higher grades of professional and technical personnel, whether or not they belong to the Party. These people go wherever their superiors may assign them, just as the junior executives of a big American corporation get shifted from one branch office to another. This kind of compulsion certainly isn't very burdensome; at least a man knows what is ahead of him when he applies for Party membership or professional training, and presumably accepts the consequences of his own free will.

A little tougher is the case of certain lower-grade workers in which the government has an investment. If a man has been given a university education, for example, he has to pay for it by working in an assigned job for at least a few years after graduation. (I knew one student in Kiev University who worried constantly for fear she would be sent to some post in Siberia, far away from the young man she hoped to marry.) People in this group, however—like the Party members and professional men—often have friends in high places who can help them wangle a congenial assignment.

Still worse off are the young people who are compelled to take industrial training in the so-called trade schools. Some of them volunteer, but the majority are arbitrarily selected by local officialdom—usually the governing council of a collective farm—to be sent away for apprenticeship. In Dnepropetrovsk I saw about four hundred and fifty of these students at work in a shoe factory. Their ages ranged from thirteen to sixteen. They worked four hours a day and spent four more in vocational-education classes. For this they were paid about eight dollars a month, plus board and lodging in a rather grim-looking hostel about a block away from the factory. The equipment they worked with was primitive, since the Germans had taken all of the plant's original machinery, but at the time I was there the students were turning out better than a thousand pairs of heavy, low-quality work shoes every day. The educational value of their work didn't seem to be particularly high, since most of them were merely repeating over and over a single set of motions which any bright youngster could learn in fifteen minutes. Compulsory education or conscript child labor? I don't know. Perhaps something in between.

In emergencies large numbers of Soviet citizens are drafted for special jobs—harvesting wheat, clearing up rubble, rafting timber during the spring thaw, grading roads, or perhaps helping to build a community clubhouse or hospital. Occasionally this is called "voluntary" work, but the social pressure (if nothing more) is so great that few people dare refuse. Perhaps the closest American parallel is the road work which is still demanded of all residents in some rural communities, or the emergency enlistment of every able-bodied man in the neighborhood to help fight a forest fire. In Russia, though, the emergencies come more often and last longer.

Finally, the political prisoners in the NKVD concentration camps represent forced labor in its most naked aspect. Some American apologists for Communism have argued that these prisoners are merely undergoing "rehabilitation through work," and that once they have done sufficient penance they can win release. (Provided, of course, that they survive the rigors of their labor.) At best, however, this argument leads to the conclusion that political prisoners are only temporary slaves, rather than slaves for life.

Since the tide turned at the battle of Stalingrad, the Russians also have been using a considerable number of German prisoners on forced labor. In the Ukraine alone, where they were doing a large part of the reconstruction work, there must have been several hundred thousand of these prisoners—although I was never able to get any official figures. Some of my Russian friends mentioned two million as a rough estimate of the total employed throughout the USSR.

They are handled by a special agency, which rents them out to municipalities and construction trusts at a rate of twenty rubles a day—about two dollars—for each laborer. Out of this sum, the contracting agency feeds and houses its wards and pays them a nominal wage, which can be used to buy tobacco and other petty luxuries. Their rations are the same as those allotted to Russian heavy laborers—eight hundred grams of black rye bread a day, plus at least one hot meal, usually some kind of stew. Their barracks are not much worse than the overcrowded apartment of the average Russian, and in cold weather they are issued Red Army overcoats and fur-lined hats in place of the flimsier Reichswehr winter clothes. They certainly did not look emaciated, and the few to whom I talked (in English or German, without any interference by their guards) claimed no ill treatment.

Yet they were the most spiritless, disheartened human beings I have ever seen. Usually they worked in gangs of about platoon strength, under the supervision of their own noncommissioned officers. The Russian guards—often merely a couple of buxom militia girls with tommy guns slung from their shoulders—paid no attention whatever to the work in hand, which proceeded at a pace that would

make a WPA crew look like a model of whirlwind efficiency. I have seen seven Germans carrying a single plank
which any one of them could have managed with one hand.
A gang worked on a half-wrecked building near my office
for five days before I could tell whether they were repair-
ing it or tearing it down. At the end of the day they would
plod back to their barracks like lost souls, eyes vacuous and
shoulders slumped. They weren't going anywhere. Many
of them had been prisoners for three years, and they had no
idea when they would go home or whether any home
would be left for them to return to.

Nearly all Soviet executives who used German laborers
were dissatisfied with them. Laziness was the usual complaint. One mayor told me: "The only way we could make
them do an honest day's work is with a club—and that we
can't do or we would be as bad as the Nazis." Other managers complained that the Germans were too fussy and
painstaking; they insisted on doing every job with a Teu-
tonic thoroughness which the Russians found madden-
ingly tedious. (In my Kiev hotel a gang of prisoners
worked for several weeks on minor repairs to the woodwork and plumbing. Their pace was certainly leisurely,
but their craftsmanship was the best I saw anywhere in
the Ukraine.) Repeatedly I was told that the Germans
didn't earn their keep, and that the labor contracts would
not be renewed—unless orders to renew came down from
the Kremlin.

For a time several thousand Rumanian prisoners worked
in the Odessa area, but they were released when the Soviet
government started wooing Rumania. This disgusted the

people of Odessa; the Rumanians had fought in that sector during the war and had earned even more hatred than the Germans. If the local residents could have had their way, the prisoners would have stayed there forever. In Dnepropetrovsk and Zaporozhe I saw a few thousand Hungarians, mostly employed on rebuilding the great steel mills of those two cities.

Only perfunctory efforts were being made, so far as I could discover, to propagandize the prisoners. Signs painted with Communist slogans—"Hitler is destroyed, but a greater Leader, Stalin, still lives" and "To the Communist Party we owe our victory"—were posted around many of their barracks, but several Germans told me that they had neither been given leaflets nor subjected to political lectures. Probably the Russians were too practical to waste their time; certainly the prisoners were in no mood for easy conversion.

It may have been significant that in all the Ukraine I never saw a German officer, or even a piece of the readily recognizable officers' uniform. One prisoner told me that the officers of his company had been marched away immediately after surrender and had not been seen again. They may, of course, have been interned in special camps in some other part of Russia.

CHAPTER
TEN

THE HAPPY PEASANT

Aside from the ruling class, the farmers appear to be better off at the moment than anybody else in the Ukraine. They eat better than city people. Their homes are more comfortable. They don't have to work as hard. The Russian farmers are, in fact, probably the only ones in the world who work an eight-hour day.

Moreover, they have a little more independence than industrial laborers. One reason is that neither police nor Party can keep the thousands of scattered peasant villages under such tight control as they do the more compact population of the cities. Another is the fact that the government is a trifle nervous about the peasants and finds it expedient to pamper them.

For the peasants, when aroused, are capable of a passive resistance which is more dangerous than any other kind of internal opposition the Party is likely to face. A strike can be easily broken; disgruntled bureaucrats can be purged; but if the farmers decide to quit producing food for the cities, there is very little the Kremlin can do about it. Twice since the Revolution—in 1920 and again in 1933— the peasants have done precisely that, and both times the blow shook the Communist regime clear down to its heels. Even today the country has not altogether recovered from the catastrophe of 1933, when the farmers slaughtered at least half of the livestock in Russia in their revolt against Stalin's scheme to force them onto collective farms.

Another such spasm of passive resistance seems unlikely in the predictable future. For one thing, the government now has a firmer grip on the machinery of agricultural production. What is more important, the collective-farm program has worked out pretty well, so that the peasants are now relatively prosperous and content. Much of the documentary evidence indicates that up until now they have profited from the Revolution more than any other major group.

Their biggest gain has been in social status. Until the Revolution the peasant was a second-class citizen, or worse. Only a short time before, he had been a serf, bound to a specific tract of land and sold with it like the cherry trees or fence posts. Even after serfdom was legally abolished, he remained at the foot of the social ladder—much like a freed slave in Mississippi after the Civil War. He did all the dirty work, took the sneers and snubs, and was expected to stay in his place. He alone could legally be punished by flogging—and the whip was laid on for countless minor offenses.

Some traces of this ago-old tradition of inferiority still hang on, in spite of the Revolution. I have heard city people—good Communists—speak of peasants with a sort of automatic condescension, taking it for granted that they were probably stupid and certainly uncouth. Nevertheless, the farmer stands a long notch higher in public esteem than he did in czarist days. The newspapers praise him, and politicians constantly assure him that he has become an important fellow. His children can go to the university, and he himself can become a colonel, a factory foreman, or a county political boss, if only he shows the necessary energy and ambition. He also has a feeling—however illusory —of taking some part in the management of affairs, both for his village and for the nation. The resulting sense of a new dignity has gone a long way, I suspect, in reconciling him to many Communist notions which at first struck him as outlandish and impractical.

The peasants also are better off in material things. Their homes—in the Ukraine, at least—are much the same as they have been for the last three hundred years. The typical family of five or six lives in a two-room cabin of squared logs, plastered with clay and whitewashed inside and out. Earth is mounded about three feet high against the walls to keep out the cold, and the roof is covered with a thick straw thatch. (Some of the newer houses have roofs of galvanized iron, tile, or asphalt shingling, which are less of a fire hazard than straw but not so warm.) The small windows have double panes with improvised weatherstripping of rags or wads of cotton stuffed around their edges; on the north side, where the winter wind is strongest, there generally are no windows. A shed for the family cow and pigs may be built against the south wall, near the door. The center of the household, both physically and symbolically, is the big brick stove which serves for cooking, heat, and a warm place to sleep.

If the cottage itself is no better than it was in the old

days, the furnishings certainly are. Usually there is now a bed for the head of the household and his wife; the kids and grandma still sleep on the stove top and the floor. The unpainted wooden table, three-legged stools, and home-made clothes chest are about what you might have found before the Revolution—they may, indeed, have been in the family for three or four generations. But the sewing machine is an important addition, which means lighter work for the women and better clothes for all the family; many of the thriftier farmers bought one in the prosperous years just before the war. Perhaps there is a radio, built to a Soviet design of peculiar political efficiency. It consists merely of a loudspeaker, wired to a central receiving set which serves the whole village. This central set is located in the headquarters of the local Party secretary, who selects the programs, thus saving everybody else the trouble of tuning in for themselves. I knew one farmer who had built his own crystal set with wire and earphones he liberated from a German communications center in the course of a güerrilla raid, but I never saw a peasant home with a private set capable of catching short-wave broadcasts from abroad.

Bedbugs, fleas, and cockroaches may not have disappeared, but they are likely to be less plentiful than they were a generation ago, because the Party conducts sporadic crusades against them in the name of Soviet culture. For the same reason, the privy—often just a shallow hole in the ground—usually is now located a little farther from the house than it used to be, and the village well nearly always has a cover and built-up sides to keep out surface drainage.

Such refinements as screens and refrigeration are still un-known.

(In passing, it might be noted that for any foreign visi-tor, a trip to the collective men's room is an expedition of concern to the whole community. The proper technique is to communicate your intention to the village's Party secretary. He then ascertains which privy is most present-able, assigns a committee to escort you to it, and appoints another detail to shoo the rest of the population off to the south forty for the sake of privacy. This is necessary, since the whole village gathers as soon as a visitor arrives, and follows his every step as long as he is on the farm; then they talk about the visit for weeks after. Any such diversion is a bright point in peasant life.)

During the war many farm villages—perhaps a third of all those in the Ukraine—were burned by the Germans. (Not by the Russians; in rural areas, as well as cities, the Soviet scorched-earth policy apparently existed mostly on paper. Few peasants ever heard of it, and none of those I met claimed to have destroyed anything in advance of the Nazi invaders.) This loss is causing great suffering. For instance, at Dikanka, an uncommonly lovely little village celebrated in one of Gogol's books, only two houses were standing in the summer of 1946. Two hundred families were living in dugouts, and their fields were still pocked with shell holes and littered with ruined tanks. Through-out the republic hundreds of thousands of families are still living in the most primitive kind of dugouts and rubble shacks, reminiscent of the Hoovervilles which sprang up in many American cities during the depression. Most of them are scheduled to move into new homes before the winter of 1947, however, because logs usually are available from the village woodlot and the job of rebuilding is much simpler than in the cities.

Next to bad housing, the clothing shortage is causing the most serious hardship among the peasantry. Because new textiles have been almost unavailable since 1941, the quilted peasant coats are nearly always patched and ragged, and thousands of farmers have no shoes except homemade birchbark sandals. Fortunately the majority of families managed to save some spare clothing, kitchenware, and bedding from the Germans. Their country has been invaded with such regularity that they long ago worked out a traditional method for forestalling looters. Every farmer has a hideaway—a pit under the kitchen floor or a concealed cave in the woods—where the valuables are tucked away at the first sign of an approaching column. Some of these safe-deposit boxes, I was told, have been kept ready for instant use ever since the wars of the Crimean Khans nearly four hundred years ago. They are ready even now. They have become a sort of concrete expression of the peasant's expectation of war, kept alive today by the fears and deliberate propaganda of the government.

One enrichment which the long procession of invaders left behind was a lot of good recipes. The Ukrainian women picked up a few tips on cooking from every race that moved across their land, with the result that they now set the most varied and appetizing tables in Russia. Black bread, with a strong, sourish flavor that I grew to like, is the mainstay, but a well-brought-up housewife can supplement it with dozens of varieties of soups, dumplings, and *variniki*, a local delicacy which resembles ravioli stuffed with cheese. She's likely to keep a jug of vodka tucked away for feast days, too. Although its manufacture is supposed to be a state monopoly, a good many farmers distill a few liters on the sly. Their word for it, curiously enough, can be literally translated as "moonshine."

Farm cooking in the Ukraine not only is better than anywhere else in the USSR; it also is a cut above any I've ever eaten on American farms, aside from a few Texas cattle ranches and Pennsylvania Dutch homesteads. Moreover, I was surprised to find that the over-all standard of living—although still way below that of Iowa, Illinois, or Pennsylvania farmers—is considerably higher than that of the average share-cropper in our Southern cotton states.

Evidently I was not alone in my surprise. Alexei Gregorovich Koval, who runs the agricultural department of the Poltava region, told me a story—after we had got pretty well acquainted during several days of travel together—about another foreign visitor whom he identified only as "an erudite Englishwoman."

"She came to Poltava just before the war," he said, "when our region had frequent visitors from abroad. They were routed here because this is one of the finest wheat districts in all Russia. And I got in the bad habit of taking all of them to see the same two or three collective farms.

"I didn't really mean to deceive anybody. Those farms were good ones, but not much above average. The peasants there had learned how to behave before company, though, and how to show their places off. It just seemed easier to keep on coming back whenever I had a foreign guest to take around.

"This Englishwoman—a very learned type—noticed that my pet farmers seemed to be a bit too well trained, and she got suspicious. One day when we were driving back from such an inspection she accused me of fooling her, and demanded that I let her pick out the next place to visit. A few minutes later we passed a cottage where, it so happened, I had never been myself. And she said: 'I want to stop there.'

"I was pretty nervous. It was a little after dinnertime, and I thought it would be just my luck for us to find the place littered with dirty dishes, the farmer curled up drunk in a corner, and his wife shaking bedbugs out of the quilt. But, thank God, it turned out to be a nice, clean house. Better yet, the peasant was a fine old fellow with a beard like Tolstoy's—and he was sitting in a rocking chair reading a copy of the Moscow *Pravda* aloud to his wife. She was working away on a brand new sewing machine. A very cultured spectacle.

"The Englishwoman got more suspicious than ever. She thought that somehow I must have fooled her again. She wouldn't even believe that the old man really subscribed to a Moscow newspaper until he showed a stack of back issues. For the next three days she kept me busy taking her to farmhouses which she pointed out at random. Not all of them were as good as that first one—but in the end I think she was convinced that our people lived pretty well."

Koval brought the story up, I suspect, because I had shown a certain skepticism myself, and had asked to plan my own inspection trip just as the Englishwoman had. He agreed readily enough, and put no obstacles in the way of my seeing the bad along with the good. Koval himself was fairly impressive testimony for Soviet agriculture—a well-trained agronomist, with a sensitive, intellectual face and a lively curiosity about American farming methods. His job corresponded, roughly, to that of a county agricultural extension agent in the United States, and I'm confident that he would have measured up pretty well to American professional standards.

His appearance, however, would have ruined him if he had ever had to deal with American farmers, for he dressed and acted like a city slicker. His only concession to the peasantry was a linen shirt, embroidered at the collar in red and blue, of the kind traditional among Cossacks. Over that he wore a neatly pressed blue serge suit and a leather coat which no farmer could ever hope to afford. His nails were carefully manicured, and his hands obviously hadn't held a plow handle or manure fork in years. In talking to the peasants, Koval was gracious and polite—but his manner made it clear that he was dispensing learning from a pedestal of authority, not speaking as one farmer to another. He belonged to the ruling class, and he was too honest to make any effort to conceal the privileges and status which his position gave him.

It is in community assets, rather than in private possessions, that the Ukrainian farm people have made their longest material strides since the Revolution. The most striking improvement—especially to an American—is in medical care. In spite of wartime setbacks, it is still better than the medical service available in the overwhelming majority of America's rural communities.

Every three or four villages have been organized into what is known as a medical section, and when the war broke out the Ukraine was well on the way toward its goal of a small hospital—fifteen or twenty beds—for each section. Many of these were razed by the Germans, but they are being rapidly rebuilt. I've watched peasants sifting through the ashes in search of a few surgical instruments to give them a start in equipping a new medical center.

Each medical section normally serves eight or ten thousand people. Its staff consists of one general physician, one dentist, and eight or nine assistants, including internes, midwives, pharmacists, and nurses. In addition to its hospital, the section usually has a drug dispensary and one or two maternity homes. A generation ago the ordinary peasant woman had her babies with no attendant except the village crone, whose only qualification was a good memory for the ancient folk superstitions. But in 1945 qualified obstetricians delivered seventy-nine per cent of all the farm babies born in the Ukraine; the rest were delivered by trained midwives.

The result has been a spectacular decline in infant mortality. Dr. Illarion Kononenko, the Ukrainian Minister of Health, showed me figures indicating that only three-and-one-half per cent of the peasant children now die before they reach the age of one year, in comparison with a fourteen per cent death rate before the Revolution. I have no reason to doubt his statistics. Certainly the youngsters were as husky as you could find anywhere.

In addition to their hospitals, most rural communities have acquired two other new assets: schools and club-houses. The school usually is a modest two- or three-room affair, and in some ravaged villages classes are being held temporarily in dugouts and farmers' kitchens; but at least the children have a better chance to learn to read and write than their parents did. The clubhouse—frequently the converted home of a czarist landlord or wealthy *kulak*— is a sort of combined center for adult education, Party propaganda, and occasional dances or song fests.

But village life is not yet the pastoral idyll often pictured in communist propaganda. An American immediately notices the absence of anything corresponding to our country stores, and the farm homes conspicuously lack the countless little items which such stores might provide. Even crockery and kitchen utensils are scarce. I once saw a farmer and his two children eating their breakfast— buckwheat mush—out of a single bowl, with hand-carved wooden spoons. Only a few villages, notably those near the Dnieper dam, have electric lights. Farm women still carry their water from a central village well in buckets slung from a wooden yoke. Telephone service reaches only the larger towns, and there it is generally limited to police and Party headquarters. And the most serious lack of all is roads. In muddy weather—which may mean four months out of the year—the typical village is as isolated today as it was three hundred years ago.

While the peasant clearly has gained something in the last twenty years, those gains were never the primary objective of Soviet farm policy. That policy, like most others, was conceived in fear of war. Its fundamental purpose was —and still is—to strengthen the Soviet Union against a possible foreign attack; any benefits to the Russian farm people are a secondary consideration. In the light of that purpose, the policy has proved a fair (but by no means complete) success.

When the Bolsheviks set out in 1930 to recast the nation's agriculture into a new collective pattern, they evidently had in mind two distinct goals, one political and the other economic. Each of these, in turn, had two parts. The political aim was, first, to wipe out some five million of the more prosperous and independent peasants—the so-called *kulaks*—who formed a hard core of latent opposition to Communism, and then to force the rest into an organizational framework which the Kremlin could more easily control. The economic aim was to increase farm production, and at the same time to shift several million workers from the land into rapidly expanding Soviet industry.

Given these objectives, the collectivization scheme made sense. It was a bloody and expensive business, but it probably was the only way in which the Politburo could accomplish all these things in a hurry. And it had to hurry, in order to build up food supplies and industry for World War II, which the Communists then confidently expected.

The political objective was reached on schedule. How the *kulaks* were disposed of within the short span of five years is now a well-known story. It was a simple process of taking their land away—and, if they objected, shipping them in cattle cars to the NKVD labor camps in Siberia. John D. Littlepage, an American engineer who was then working for the Soviet government, had a considerable force of these exiles assigned to the mines he supervised, and in his book *In Search of Soviet Gold* he has set down a melancholy record of their bewilderment and suffering.

The process by which the Communist bosses tightened their grip on the remaining peasants is less generally understood. I have not been able, in fact, to find any adequate published account of the ingenious machinery which the government has devised for making even the most remote and politically backward farmer toe the mark.

The chief cog in this mechanism, as described to me by Soviet agricultural authorities, is the Machine Tractor Station. At least one of these stations has been set up in every *raion* or county. Normally it has a pool of fifty to one hundred tractors, plus a considerable number of gang plows and combines. Its job is to do the plowing and harvesting for all the collective farms in the county. Most foreign students of Soviet agriculture have assumed that this is the only job, and have overlooked the Station's political function—which is at least equally important.

The dangerous thing about the old farming system (from the Communist viewpoint) was the almost complete independence it gave the individual peasant. He did all of his own plowing and harvesting, raised all of his food, and marketed the surplus himself. If he decided to withhold his grain from the market, because he didn't like the price or couldn't buy enough consumers' goods with the proceeds, the government was helpless—and the cities faced starvation. Nobody but the farmer himself knew how much surplus he really had, and he often showed surprising skill in concealing his little stock in hidden granaries. Both the czarist ministers and Trotsky, in the early years of the Revolution, discovered that it was virtually impossible to make forced collections of grain from these millions of secret hoards, even when they sent out armed searching parties. It was clear to the Communists that so long as the peasant possessed this power to withhold grain, he would be holding a knife at the very throat of the regime.

The Machine Tractor Station took that knife away. It knows down to the last bushel how much grain every acre produces, because all of it runs through the MTS combines and threshers. Better yet, it collects a share of the harvest on the spot, in payment for its services, and turns it in to the state granaries. (The MTS fee varies considerably, according to the crop and the yield per acre. It always is figured on a percentage basis, and I was told that in some cases it runs as high as twenty-five per cent of the total harvest.) In addition, each collective farm must sell a considerable part of its remaining produce to the government at a low fixed price. This sale is, in effect, a land rent paid in kind; and it cannot be evaded, because the Tractor Station's records are open to the government revenue agents.

It would be possible even now for disgruntled peasants to cut down on the flow of food to the cities by deliberate neglect of cultivation, or by hand reaping part of the crop at night and hiding it away. But this kind of sabotage would be relatively ineffective and easy to detect. The government is still careful not to antagonize the farmers too much; but it is far less at their mercy than it was in the old days, before they had to depend on the Machine Tractor Stations for the key agricultural operations. Indeed, so long as the government keeps firm control of the Stations, an effective peasant revolt would appear to be impossible. It would be quickly broken by hunger alone, since the peasant no longer has the livestock necessary to do his own plowing.

The Communists are never likely to lose control of the Machine Tractor Stations, because each of them is a political strong point. The director always is a staunch Party member. One of his three vice-directors is a trained political agent, charged with spreading the word throughout the country by means of the Station's influence and responsible for keeping a finger on the pulse of opinion. (The other two vice-directors are an agronomist and a machinery technician.) Moreover, the Station's entire staff is selected with an eye to political fidelity, as well as ability to handle machinery. Most of the employees are young men, the pick of the countryside, who have been thoroughly indoctrinated in the Party's youth organizations.

Naturally the government does not depend on the Machine Tractor Station as its only instrument of control. Every collective farm is dominated directly by the Party organization. The farm chairman always is a Communist —nominally elected by the entire membership of the farm, but actually designated by the county political boss. Every question brought before the farm assembly is considered first by the Party cell, made up of only three or four per cent of the collective's membership. In practice, its decision—usually guided by instruction from above—is final; the non-Party members find it prudent not to argue the point, lest they fall under suspicion of heresy. Thus in practically all cases the assembly votes unanimous approval of the Party cell's recommendations.

As extra insurance, the NKVD invariably has one or two secret informers on every farm, keeping an eye both on the ordinary peasants and the Party members. They, presumably, were largely responsible for the wholesale removal of farm managers and MTS personnel which Khrushchev put into effect throughout the Ukraine in the summer of 1946.

That purge was one indication of the effectiveness of the controls which the Party has forged since the collective farming program got under way in 1930. It kept its grip on the countryside, in the face of what seemed to be a considerable upsurge of "bourgeois nationalist" sentiment. And there was no withholding of crops on any dangerous scale.

In its economic objectives, the Soviet farm policy has been less successful. True enough, it has achieved a significant increase in farm production, and it has released hundreds of thousands of farm workers every year for industrial jobs. Yet, in comparison with the Western world, Russian agriculture is still woefully inefficient; and the collective farms still hold an astonishing reservoir of sur-plus manpower, which the government has not been able to siphon off in spite of its need for every available pair of hands.

The technical advantages of the collective-farm pro-gram are obvious. Before the Revolution, the typical peas-ant farmed a tiny plot—rarely more than fifteen or twenty acres—by hopelessly backward methods. Usually he did not live on his land, like an American farmer, but in a vil-lage some distance away; and his holding probably was not all in one piece, but divided into three or more strips which were scattered throughout the acreage belonging to his village. Moreover, he seldom had complete control of his holding. Every family head belonged to a village or-ganization called the *Mir*—a sort of town council tradi-tional in most parts of Russia since the beginnings of history—and the *Mir* held vague but extensive powers in the management of the village land. It set the dates for the beginning of planting and harvesting, for example, decreed crop rotations, and from time to time it reshuffled the strips so that every family would get a turn at the more fertile soil.

Under this system, the use of heavy farm machinery was impossible; a tractor couldn't be employed efficiently on the tiny strips, even if an individual farmer could afford one. Moreover, the smarter and more ambitious peasants couldn't adopt better methods—improved rotations, new varieties of crops, more fertilizers—because they would have disrupted the general pattern imposed by custom and the *Mir*. For these reasons, a number of czarist reformers

(Peter Stolypin was the best known) tried to encourage the "strong and sober" peasants to separate their land from the village holdings and set up as independent farmers. A few did, and thus became the *kulaks* whom the Communists wiped out a generation later. But in general the old pattern persisted up until 1930.

The great Soviet reform which began in that year simply lumped all the village land together and converted it into a collective farm—bringing back into it whatever acreage the *kulaks* had split away as the result of Stolypin's legislation. As Sir John Maynard has pointed out, this step was a far less drastic break with tradition than it would have been in England or America. The *Mir* which always had exercised a quasi-communal authority over the village land, was easily transformed into a village-soviet. The real innovation was technical—the tilling of the combined acreage in one piece, instead of many small strips, by means of modern equipment. This meant that many other scientific improvements could be introduced for the first time. It insured prompt completion of each farming operation at the right moment, thus cutting down on the wastage through late planting or a delayed harvest. (Hand reaping, for example, took days of bone-cracking toil; and if a storm blew up during these days, it might knock half the ripe grain out of the wheat ears.) It enabled the collectives to make use of the services of trained agronomists, as the individual peasants never could. Most important of all, the large-scale introduction of machinery resulted in great savings in labor. To the planners in the Kremlin, all this

no doubt sounded pretty wonderful; and much of it turned
out to be almost as good as it sounded.

Nevertheless, the collective farming program ran into
tough going at the start—and its troubles are not yet over.
The *kulaks*, of course, didn't like the idea. Many of them
killed their livestock and broke their tools rather than turn
them over to the lazier and less thrifty peasants who made
up the majority of the collective. The removal of the
kulaks was in itself a blow to agriculture, since they were
—by definition—the most intelligent and enterprising
members of their communities. Even the poorer peasants
slaughtered their cattle in large numbers—because, Maynard suggests, they naïvely assumed that the government
would stock the new collective farms, and they figured
they might as well have a good feed of meat before the
New Order started. For whatever reason, livestock disappeared by the millions, and Russia has been on short meat
rations ever since.

In fact, the peasants have never become fully reconciled
to the collective ownership of livestock. There was no
precedent for it comparable to the tradition of the *Mir*,
which was so easily adapted to collective ownership of the
land. Moreover, the relation of a farmer to his animals
always is a peculiarly personal one, as anybody familiar
with American agriculture can testify. At any rate, after
a few years of stubborn experiment, the Communists
backtracked. They gave every family a garden plot of its
own, quite separate from the collective acreage. This tract,
normally one to three acres, lies close by the peasant's

house. It is strictly private property; whatever vegetables
and livestock he can raise there belong to him alone, subject
to the usual taxes. And today at least seventy per cent of all
the cows in the Ukraine are raised on these garden plots
under private ownership. Before the war the percentage
was somewhat lower; but the collective herd suffered
greater wartime losses. When a peasant had to choose between saving his own livestock or that belonging to the
collective farm, it nearly always was his cow which he
drove off to the swamp, while the commonly owned cattle
got left in the barn for the hungry Germans.

The restoration of a degree of private ownership went
a long way toward converting the peasants to the Soviet
farm policy. But it has proved a constant source of trouble.
Nearly everywhere the farmers have shown an incurable
tendency to lavish more time and sweat on their own little
gardens than on the collective acreage. This is noticeable
even to the casual visitor; everywhere I went in the
Ukraine, the individual gardens were the neatest and most
carefully tended part of the collective farms.

Furthermore, the sinful instincts of private property die
hard. As the 1946 purge of the agricultural administration
revealed, many peasants have managed to enlarge their
own holdings at the collective's expense, by such simple
devices as moving the boundary posts a few inches at a
time on dark nights. Even some farm managers (now
liquidated) winked at the diversion of collective property
—seed, tools, and fertilizer—to use on the private tracts.
Pravda reported that an incomplete check-up in the
Kuibyshev region alone had turned up 11,760 cases in the

first six months of 1946 where state property had been misused and personal gardens illegally enlarged.

Another difficult problem has been the lush growth of bureaucracy in the administration of the collective farms. When I was traveling through rural areas in the spring of 1946, I marveled at the number of supervisors, bookkeepers, agronomists, and miscellaneous technicians who seemed to be involved in the management of Ukrainian agriculture; and a few months later the Communist Party Control Committee noted that the same thing was true elsewhere. It issued a stern decree condemning the "unfoundedly swollen administrative staffs of many collective farms, which results in . . . many idlers on service jobs who are doing nothing and receive higher pay than farmers engaged in production," and it ordered criminal prosecution of the guilty officials. Whether such measures can cure what seems to be an inherent weakness of the collective farming scheme is open to considerable question.

Finally—for some reason I've never been able to understand—Ukrainian agriculture has not made the technical progress which seems to be easily within its grasp. It has the technicians; I've done enough farm work myself to tell that the agronomists whom I met in the Ukraine knew their business. Russian soil scientists—Dokuchaiev, Glinka, Praslov, and many others—are recognized by our own Department of Agriculture as leaders in their field. Many of the individual farm managers had all the earmarks of good farmers anywhere, plus a lively enthusiasm for their jobs. Yet, according to the government's own records, the USSR has not achieved any marked increase in production per acre. The total farm output has risen sharply—grain crops, for example, climbed from about 67,000,000 tons in 1928 to 118,000,000 in 1940. But this is almost entirely the result of planting more acres. The yield per acre is still about thirteen bushels, or very slightly more than it was in 1913. Even this figure must be accepted with considerable skepticism, since Russian official agricultural statistics are notoriously optimistic. (Frequently they are based merely on a survey of the standing ripe grain, without any allowance for wastage in harvest.) My own guess, after considerable study and discussion with individual farmers, is that the Ukrainian grain harvest in 1945 could not have exceeded eight to ten bushels per acre, and that in 1946 (because of drought) it was considerably lower.

A partial explanation for the low yields may be soil exhaustion. Russia's land has been heavily cropped for centuries, and the Soviets have not yet been able to manufacture anything like enough artificial fertilizer to restore it. Moreover, the replacement of horses by tractors has sharply cut the supply of natural manure. Another partial explanation is low rainfall—seldom more than eighteen inches in the best farming sections of the Ukraine.

Yet when all such allowances have been made, it is still clear that Russian farming is curiously—and unnecessarily —behind the times. Virtually nothing, for example, has been done to check soil erosion. Thousands of acres have been badly gullied or scalped by sheet erosion, as any plane traveler cannot help but notice. But I never saw a single terrace or check dam anywhere in western Russia. Even contour plowing is entirely unknown. Windbreaks have been planted here and there, but they are still rarities. Hybrid corn has not been introduced on a commercial scale, and artificial insemination is only now coming into use by livestock breeders. Soviet research centers have made some spectacular experiments in developing new plants, such as colored cotton; but so far as I could learn, only the new perennial wheat is likely to have much economic significance in the near future.

The surplus manpower which is still dammed up on Ukrainian farms is equally surprising to an outsider; but it is not quite so hard to guess at an explanation.

The Russian land always has been overmanned; and by our standards it is today. The typical collective farm in the Ukraine includes about 1,800 acres. It is worked by an average of 250 able-bodied adults—that is, one farm hand for every seven acres. (On the same kind of wheat land in Texas and Oklahoma, it is not unusual for one man to handle seventy-five to a hundred acres, or more.) At one farm, I met four men who had nothing to do except take care of twenty-four horses. At another, two women were detailed full time to look after twelve cows. Elsewhere I ran across one old lady who made a career of tending one goat—but that was an exceptional case.

Naturally, so many people can't keep very busy. All the American farmers I've known have a grisly habit of getting up long before dawn and working until after dark; but the Russian collective farmer puts in an eight-hour day. His spare time is devoted to his own garden, to the study of veterinary medicine or Marxist theory in the village clubhouse, or maybe just to plain loafing. More leisure for farm people anywhere is a fine thing—but, in such generous helpings, it seems like a strange luxury for a country in the grip of a severe manpower shortage.

Perhaps it looks like an expensive luxury to the Communists, too; but it is hard for them to do anything about it. The political objections to increasing the farmer's working hours beyond those of the industrial laborer are obvious. In addition, an abnormal supply of manpower is necessary, for the moment, on the farms of western Russia, because the Germans destroyed nearly all of the mechanical equipment. Before the war the Ukraine had about one hundred thousand tractors. In 1946 only forty thousand were in service. Most of these were rickety affairs, pieced together out of parts taken from wrecked machines; the rest had been sent in from eastern Russia or from occupied enemy territory. A severe gasoline shortage also hampered mechanized farm operations in 1945 and 1946.

As a result, cattle had to haul the plows over millions of acres of Ukrainian land. This practice, incidentally, sharply cut down milk production, and caused a good deal of grumbling among the peasants. No horses were available except those too scrubby for the Germans to steal, plus a few rejects from the Red Army cavalry. These were nearly all shaggy Siberian ponies, not much bigger than a Shetland, and every one I saw was gaunt and wobbly. Since neither the few tractors nor the scant available livestock could do all the plowing, a good deal of land had to be turned over with spades. That back-breaking work was largely done by women. Something over sixty per cent of the laborers on collective farms are women, and they get no favors when the work is being assigned.

Even with every cow, pony, and housewife in the fields, it was not possible to plow more than seventy per cent of normal Ukrainian acreage in 1946, and some of that was not harvested. An uncommonly severe drought cut production still further; and it was evident to nearly everybody—long before Stalin made the announcement—that the government's plan for abolishing bread rationing would have to be postponed. Under such circumstances, it plainly will be impossible to shift many farm workers into industry until the stock of tractors is replaced. That probably cannot be accomplished before 1949.

A final reason for the swollen farm population is simply that people don't want to leave just now. On the farms they can raise plenty to eat, in normal crop years at least; their houses are more comfortable and less overcrowded than city homes; and even if they could earn more money in the factories, there isn't much to buy with it. Consequently, the peasants are not likely to move into industry in any considerable numbers these days, unless the government forces them. And it is probably a safe bet that the government will not try large-scale compulsion on the peasantry until its manpower shortage becomes very acute, indeed. The scars of the last such attempt are still too fresh.

Consequently, it is plain that Soviet farm policy still is a long way from its goals. It is not yet producing enough food to meet the normal peacetime demand, much less to build up war reserves, and it is not yet funneling the maximum number of peasant laborers into the new war industries. Under the circumstances, however, it has done surprisingly well, and no prudent observer would care to gamble that the goals will not be met by the end of the next Five Year Plan.

CHAPTER
ELEVEN

WHAT ARE THEY
UP TO?

IN THE FOREGOING CHAPTERS WE HAVE SEEN HOW Soviet resources—land, industry, and people—are being channeled into preparations for war. It seems a reasonable guess, from the evidence at hand, that the primary reason for these preparations is an ingrained fear of attack from abroad. But can we be sure that is the *only* reason? Isn't it possible that the men in the Kremlin may themselves be planning an aggressive war to conquer the world for Communism?

We have to find some kind of answer to that question. Until we do, it is impossible for us to work out any sensible foreign policy of our own. For this reason, it may well be the most important question our generation will ever have to face. Our answer may decide not only whether we shall be seared to death in an atomic war, but whether the whole Western concept of freedom and self-government goes down with us.

It would be easy to argue that the Soviet war preparations are not merely defensive but are aimed at an eventual campaign of conquest. That theory would seem to square with events inside the country just as well as the theory of fear. It also would provide a plausible explanation for many of the Soviet Union's recent actions abroad. It can be supported with texts from the sacred writings of Marxism, which certainly preach that the whole world must someday yield to Communism. Moreover, this theory fits the inflamed anti-Soviet prejudices of many Americans—both extreme conservatives and disillusioned leftists. A number of them, indeed, have already seized upon it as a complete answer to the question which Senator Vandenberg once asked in such exasperated bewilderment: "What is Russia up to?"

But this is an answer which no prudent and responsible man can accept in a hurry, for it is the answer of despair. If we once decide that the Soviet Union is heading for world domination, there could be only one logical course for America to follow: that is, to attack first. Moreover, we ought to attack now, while we have the atom bomb and they still do not. If war is inevitable, we had better fight it soon, because our chance of victory shrinks with every day we wait.

Plainly that is a course we can adopt only if we are certain—beyond any whisper of doubt—that there is no alternative. The American people will never be persuaded to fight a preventive war unless they have overwhelming proof that the conflict cannot be avoided. (Perhaps not even then. We hung back in 1940, when Hitler's intentions had become pretty obvious.) And so far we have no absolutely conclusive evidence that Russia is dead set toward aggression.

Neither do we have conclusive proof that she is not. Personally, I think it probable that fear really is the mainspring of Soviet behavior, and that the Kremlin is following what it believes to be a purely defensive policy. Yet that is at best a guess, and we cannot afford to act as if it were a certainty.

If we could be certain, then America's only sensible line of action would be to do everything in our power to remove that fear. That would mean handing over the atom-bomb secrets with no strings attached. It would mean clearing out of nearly all the military outposts we have just won at such cost of blood and taxes. It would mean the scrapping of our unwritten alliance with Great Britain and the abandonment of most of Europe and Asia to Soviet domination. In short, it would mean throwing away our main defenses—for the Russian leaders have made it clear that they will not (at present) accept anything less as a satisfactory guarantee of their security.

But this is a course we dare not pursue so long as there is any doubt whatever about Russia's intentions. If it should turn out that we had guessed wrong, and the Soviet Union should start a campaign of aggression after all, then we would find that we had doomed ourselves to almost sure defeat. We cannot afford to drop our guard on the strength of a guess.

If both of these answers must be rejected, there is still a third choice. We can acknowledge frankly that it is not now possible to arrive at a sure and final answer to the question: What is Russia up to?—and we can then adopt a working hypothesis that will cover both possibilities. We can assume that the Russians *probably* are behaving in their present disturbing fashion because they are afraid; but that they *may* be getting ready to try to impose Communism on the rest of the world by force.

On an assumption of that kind, is it possible to build an American policy which holds some reasonable promise of peace? I think it is. It will be a long, tough, disagreeable job; it will be expensive; it will demand more patience and steadiness than we, as a nation, have ever shown before. But it should not be impossible.

To begin with, we'll have to recognize that nothing we can safely do at the moment will entirely dispel the Soviet fears. We must expect the present mistrust and tension to continue for a considerable period. During that period we must follow a line of action which will keep us strong against any possible attack and which at the same time will be calculated to prove to the Russians—eventually—that they have nothing to fear from us. That may not be as hard as it sounds because (as we shall see a little later) the same measures needed to keep us strong may also serve, over the course of years, to wipe out the Soviet misgivings.

Let's examine, first, the framework within which such a policy will have to be built. Then we can see a little more clearly the shape of the policy itself.

For a while a good many of us hoped that the United Nations might provide the framework for a firm structure of security. It has now become mournfully apparent, however, that the UN isn't going to work out that way. It may still prove very useful as an arena for negotiation—but it cannot serve, by itself, as the basic pattern of world organization.

For the men who run the Soviet Union have shown unmistakably, in every move they have made since the end of the war, that they don't take the United Nations really seriously. They are willing to play along with it, because it offers a useful sounding board for their propaganda—and, after all, it can do them no harm so long as they hold their veto. But up to this writing they have refused to have anything to do with its chief operating agencies—the International Bank, the Stabilization Fund, the Food and Agriculture Organization, and the conferences dealing with international trade and aviation. They have refused to discuss seriously a strong United Nations police force. They have stalled, up to now, all plans for the effective international control of atomic energy. They have made it plain, in other words, that they are not willing to rely on the United Nations as their main line of defense.

The reason, I think, is that Russians do not believe the United Nations would be any more effective in stopping an aggressive America—once it had turned "fascist" and "imperialist"—than the League of Nations was capable of halting an aggressive Germany. They suspect that it might even turn into a grand alliance against the Soviet Union, because the Western democracies hold a majority in the UN—and they nearly always vote solidly together. So long as it might be dominated by what they regard as potential enemies, the Russians feel that they cannot safely put their trust in any world-wide association of nations. (Much

less in a real world government, that wistful dream of so
many American idealists.)

Consequently, the Soviet leaders are determined to organize their own security on quite a different pattern. It
is a simple pattern, built out of three main pieces:

1. A strong Red Army, backed up by a war industry
at least equal to any in the world.

2. A protective belt of satellite states, under firm Soviet
control, outside of every vulnerable frontier.

3. Constant efforts to weaken and divide their potential
enemies—the Western democracies—by every weapon of
diplomacy and propaganda.

The most useful tools for the latter purpose are, of
course, the local Communist parties in each of the Western
nations. Thus the American Communists opposed our loan
to Britain; and so did the British Communists, although in
the interests of plausibility they had to use quite different
arguments. The French Communists fight bitterly to prevent any close understanding between France and England. The Latin-American Communists rail noisily against
"Yanqui imperialism." And so on, wherever you care to
look in the Western world, the native Communists make
it their first task to support the USSR and to undermine
the foreign policies of their own countries. They also provide recruits for the Soviet espionage network, as the
Canadian spy investigation revealed. And it is noteworthy
that in every Western nation they have concentrated on
filtering into the transport and communications unions,
where they could cause the maximum amount of sabotage
and disruption in time of war.

Within their security zone, on the other hand, the Russians are systematically squeezing out every remnant of Western influence—political, cultural, and economic. In most of their satellite nations all political parties have been dragooned into a Communist-directed United Front; any party that refuses to join is labeled "fascist" and outlawed. (In eastern Germany the process has not yet gone quite that far. Groups which balked at being swallowed up by the Soviet-sponsored Unity Party are still permitted to exist, but they have great difficulty in getting newsprint for their papers, halls for their speakers, and transport for their organizers. Moreover, their local leaders have developed an unaccountable habit of disappearing in the dead of night.) Because the puppet governments sometimes were wobbly and shy on public support—notably in Poland and Rumania—they needed the support of Russian arms until they could get firmly settled in the saddle. Consequently, the Soviets stalled the drafting of the peace treaties as long as possible, so they would have an excuse for leaving troops in the occupied countries. Meanwhile, they made a neighborly loan of NKVD men to help the puppet regimes organize their own political police.

Western cultural influences are being eliminated either by direct censorship or by denying paper, presses, and radio facilities to any expression of "decadent bourgeois ideas." So far this process has developed rather unevenly. In Czechoslovakia, for example, American books still circulate freely, and Western statesmen frequently are quoted in the press, while Yugoslavia has clamped down the lid so tightly that our embassy was forced to close (at least temporarily) its official information service. Throughout all of eastern Europe, nevertheless, the propaganda against American and British ideas is sustained and powerful; and the propaganda for Russian culture is equally methodical. Even the new alliance between the Kremlin and the Orthodox Church is being turned to good account.

Economic influence, to the Communists' way of thinking, is most dangerous of all, since they regard it as the key to influence of all other types. They are making especially vigorous efforts, therefore, to wipe out Western investments and trade in every country within the Soviet orbit, and to substitute their own.

One device is simply confiscation of investments, on grounds that they had been used by the Germans or Japanese and therefore had become fair game for Russian seizure as reparations. On this pretext the Soviets have taken over the considerable American oil properties in Rumania; the Opel automobile factories in Germany, entirely owned by General Motors, the Berlin electric equipment plant owned by International General Electric, and dozens of similar industrial firms which belonged to American and British investors. Manchuria was virtually stripped of its industry, mostly Chinese owned, in the same summary fashion.

Another technique is the forced partnership. The Hungarian government, for instance, was persuaded to sign—most reluctantly—a treaty providing for the sale to the USSR of half the stock in all the nation's important corporations. In payment Russia is supposed to supply raw materials to these same industries; the resulting products, in large part, will go to the Soviet Union as reparations. Another treaty of the same sort has put the Soviet Union into partnership with China in the operation of the Chinese Eastern railway, which is the economic bloodstream of Manchuria and which controls many subsidiary industries.

Still another method of economic penetration is the seizure of land and factories to support the Red armies which occupy former enemy territory. This one has been used most effectively in Austria and Korea.

In order to shut out Western commerce, most of the satellite countries have made foreign trade a state monopoly—and the bulk of the business which once went to British, French, and American firms is now kept within the Soviet family. For the same reason, the Danube—the great trade artery of eastern Europe—has been interrupted at the Bavarian border, and Russia has done everything in its power to prevent the reopening of traffic with the West. Land routes also are being reoriented toward the USSR, by such means as the new rail junction at Bratislava and the highway and rail links now under construction across Ruthenia. Even the long struggle over Trieste hinged on a question of transport at least as much as on the more publicized political and strategic issues. For Trieste is the natural port for Austria and the Balkan hinterland, and in Slav hands it would have strengthened immeasurably the Communist economic control over this area.

Soviet military dominance in the satellite states has been established as a matter of course. Red Army missions are helping to reorganize the armed forces of the puppet governments, and where necessary (as in Poland and Yugo-

slavia) equipment also has been provided. At certain
strategic points, such as the Albanian border, Russian engineers are building fortifications, airfields, and coastal
batteries. There have even been some reports, apparently
authentic, that Albania has secretly turned over to the
USSR the strategic island of Saseno for use as a major
bomber base.

The frontiers of the Russian security zone—the line
across the narrow waist of Europe from Stettin to Trieste,
for example, and the Thirty-eighth Parallel in Korea—
are guarded as vigilantly as the borders of a country at
war. Neither goods nor people can move across the line
without long delays and a great shuffling of documents,
and the innocents who sometimes wander over unawares
are promptly popped into jail as spies.

The result of all this is a new pattern of world organization which we can never like. Here is not the One World
we had hoped for but two; not the United Nations we had
intended but two groups of nations which are anything
but united. The Russian concept of security has split the
world squarely into halves, and we are shut out of the Red
half.

This violates a principle to which America is deeply
committed—the principle of free movement of trade and
ideas, without discrimination, among all nations. It also
violates our sense of fairness, for we cannot shut the Communists out of our half of the world. If we tried, we would
have to develop a political police of our own, suppress
Communist publications, clamp down an iron censorship,

outlaw suspect political parties—in short, scrap our democracy and behave just like the Russians. (In passing, it should be noted that this situation does not strike the Russians as unfair. One Soviet official argued that it would be an unfriendly act for the United States to beam short-wave broadcasts into the USSR, although the Soviet Union feels entirely free to broadcast its propaganda to America. "A perfect example of reciprocity," he explained. "Your laws provide for free speech, and we observe them. Our laws do *not*, and it would be improper for you to disregard them.")

What hurts worst of all is the feeling that we have somehow been cheated. We tried to free the little nations of eastern Europe from Nazi dictatorship, and we now find them under a Communist dictatorship that looks very much the same. We thought we had reached an agreement with the Russians, at Yalta, Moscow, and Potsdam, for democratic governments in these nations, but their idea of "democratic" turned out to be quite different from ours. We have moaned, protested, and sent diplomatic notes by the bushel, all without much result. The Red Army is there; and so is its definition of democracy.

Finally, we have had thrust upon us heavy responsibilities which we are reluctant to carry. When the world split in two, the United States inevitably became the center of one half, just as Russia became the center of the other. Since America is the only power with economic and military strength to match the USSR, all the nations outside the Soviet orbit automatically looked to us for leadership and support. Thus we found ourselves the unwilling head of that loose group of thirty-odd countries usually described as the Western democracies—although the term is by no means precise. (Some of them—China, Argentina, Saudi Arabia—are not yet democracies; nor are they all Western, either in geography or culture.)

This was a disagreeable shock to all our instincts and traditions. We would have greatly preferred to avoid such entangling alliances, tend to our own knitting, and let the rest of the world look after itself. We felt much like a confirmed bachelor who suddenly had a large, nervous, and unruly family dumped on his lap. Some of our newly acquired dependents are hungry, others have deplorable manners, and a few badly need delousing. Yet on America's shoulders—because they are strongest—rests the main responsibility for holding the family together and nursing its ailing members back to health. If we fail to take care of them, we can be sure they will move over to the Soviet household next door—and we would then stand weakened and alone.

We have many good reasons, then, for disliking this new pattern which the Russians have forced upon the world. There is no use pretending that we will ever like it. But in the end we are going to have to accept it.

We'll have to accept it because we have no other choice. So long as the Soviet leaders believe that an attack from the West is inevitable, they are not going to give up their kind of security. No amount of argument will change their minds, as Byrnes, Bevin & Company discovered during months of weary pleading. And no form of pressure, short of a full-scale war, can force them around to our way of thinking. Whether we like it or not, they have set the framework within which America must work out its own policy.

At the moment it is not a very stable framework. Some of the smaller nations have not yet been drawn firmly into the orbit of either of the Super-Powers. They are being tugged both ways, by a sort of Law of Political Gravity, like small planets caught between two great stars. These areas are the danger spots. They will remain so until they are finally pulled into the strategic zone either of America or of the USSR. Meanwhile, relations between the United States and the Soviets will remain tense, and from time to time quite possibly will get a good deal worse than they are now.

There is no prospect that the tugging contest can be ended any time soon, because the Russians believe that their protective ring of satellite countries is by no means complete. The underbelly of their vast double continent feels uncomfortably naked, as anyone can see by a glance at the map. Consequently, they would like to extend their security belt—which now runs from Finland to the Adriatic—much farther to the south and east. According to their blueprint, it should at least include Greece and its neighboring corner of the Mediterranean; Turkey, which holds the door to the Dardanelles and Black Sea; Iran, which is both the southern gateway to the great industrial area of the Urals and also a fabulous reservoir of the oil which Russia so badly needs; and perhaps additional chunks of the Middle East. In the Orient, the Soviets already hold strategic (though not complete political) con-

trol of Manchuria by virtue of their grip on the Chinese
Eastern railway and Port Arthur, and they are firmly
settled in northern Korea and the Kuriles. Very likely
they will try to swallow up all of Korea, and consolidate
their political and economic foothold in Manchuria.

For reasons noted in the next chapter, there is not a
single one of these areas which we could let slip under
Soviet domination without gravely weakening our own
security. The clash of interests, therefore, will remain
naked and unpleasant.

But it is not likely to lead to an early war. The Russians
will use every conceivable device of propaganda, political
agitation, diplomatic pressure, and military threats to gain
control over the areas they want. If these fail, however,
they will not risk a major armed struggle. For at least
fifteen years and perhaps longer they simply will not have
the strength to challenge the Western democracies at any
distance beyond their own borders. And by the time they
have built up the power for such an attempt, there is at
least a good chance of our persuading them that—if security is their only aim—further expansion is no longer
necessary.

The most serious danger, it seems to me, is that the men
in the Kremlin might get the idea that they can seize one
of these key areas without touching off a full-scale war.
If they should decide, for example, that they could march
into Turkey or Manchuria without risking a collision with
American forces, they might try it. After all, Germany
made that mistake twice: both the Kaiser and Hitler
thought they could overwhelm western Europe without

serious American opposition. They were wrong, of course; and the Russians would be equally wrong in thinking that the United States would not resist aggression against the small nations which, in the long run, are vital to the Western world.

It is up to us not to let them make such a mistake. We can no longer afford the kind of wavering and ambiguous policy which left Germany in doubt about our willingness to defend western Europe. We need to make it perfectly clear that we are committed to defend certain vital areas, that we will fight if they are invaded, and that we have the strength to fight successfully. If we draw that sort of line, we can be quite certain that the Red Army will not cross it.

CHAPTER
TWELVE

NOTES ON GETTING ALONG
WITH THE RUSSIANS

EVEN IF WE SHOULD FOOLISHLY SURRENDER THE strategic keys of both Europe and Asia, scrap the atomic bomb, give up our island bases, and abandon the other Western democracies, the men in the Kremlin still would watch us with the darkest suspicion. These gestures almost certainly would not be accepted as a permanent guarantee of America's peaceful intentions. They would not be at all likely to persuade the Russians to give up their own design for security. More probably they would be regarded as signs of weakness, symptoms of that purblind softness which is supposed to characterize "bourgeois liberal" governments.

Appeasement won't work with the Soviets any better than it did with Germany—and for a fundamental reason. The Communists simply do not take our present government seriously; they do not believe it is capable of committing the United States to any long-range course of action. In their eyes, Truman and Marshall are nice, rather fuzzy-minded old gentlemen with an honest yearning for peace—but their assurances aren't really worth much. The nice old gentlemen of pre-Hitler Germany were sincere in their pledges of friendship, too. The trouble is that those German pledges didn't hold good after Hitler came to power.

Neither would Truman's promises bind the Huey Long whom the Russians expect to stride into the White House with his own brand of American fascism during the next depression. They believe that large-scale unemployment and political upheaval are inevitable in the United States when the present boom plays out three or four years from now, and that our collapse will pull down all the countries of Latin America and western Europe which are now linked to our economy. They are sure that the American *fuehrer* who takes over then will be militantly anti-Soviet—a tool of the "reactionary financiers" whom they regard as the real bosses of the United States even now. Finally, it is one of the basic tenets of Marxism that the capitalist world can find no way out of its crisis except through imperialism and war. That is why Lenin once predicted that "a series of terrible conflicts between the Soviet Republic and the bourgeois states is unavoidable." And it should be remembered that Stalin has always prided himself on being the most faithful of Lenin's pupils.

It is hardly surprising, then, that these convictions have not been shaken by all the arguments that American diplomats have been able to muster. Indeed, nothing we can say is ever likely to budge them an inch. For the trained Communist has his own system of logic, which he believes to be infallible. Anyone who does not speak in the same terms is heard with kindly pity—much as Cardinal Spellman might listen to some Bantu tribesman reciting the virtues of devil worship.

One of my Ukrainian friends, for example, once explained to me that "since every government is merely an executive committee of the ruling class," both Congress and the White House undoubtedly are guided by some secret junta of capitalists who pull the strings from Wall Street. He was convinced that these "proto-fascists" even now must be grooming a Bilbo or Rankin or Gerald L. K. Smith to serve as their Hitler "when the next depression makes the time ripe." For the same reasons, he refused to believe that the anti-Russian crusades of the Hearst and McCormick newspapers represent only the private views of the publishers. Because both America's press and its government are controlled by The Interests, he argued, those "fascist" editorials must really be a veiled expression of official opinion. "If you had a really democratic government," he concluded, "it would wipe out those reactionary warmongers."

Moreover, the Communists are convinced that their dialectic materialism provides a crystal ball with which they can peer into the future. The official *History of the Communist Party*, published a few months ago in Moscow, puts it this way:

"The power of the Marxist-Leninist theory lies in the fact that it enables the Party to find the right orientation in any situation, to understand the inner connection of current events, to foresee their course, and to perceive not only how and in what direction they are developing in the present but how and in what direction they are bound to develop in the future."

Even General Marshall's patient reasoning can't make much of a dent on that kind of mind.

There is only one way, it seems to me, to cure the Russians of their fear of foreign attack—and it will take a long while. We simply need to pull through the next fifteen years without a major depression and without going "fascist." If we can find some democratic method of controlling the violent ups and downs of our economy—if we can hold onto full employment and our freedom at the same time—then we will have proved beyond question that the Communist forebodings are all wrong.

That kind of proof is the only sort Stalin and his associates will readily accept. Although they are impervious to mere verbal argument, they have never hesitated to reinterpret Marxist dogma whenever it collides with a hard and indisputable fact. Once they see with their own eyes that the Western nations are capable of developing a democratically controlled economy, which will neither bog down in periodic depressions nor explode into war, then they may be willing to lay their suspicions aside.

When that time comes—and, I think, not until then—the Soviets may be convinced that there is a possibility of real co-operation with the non-Communist world. They may begin to rely for security on the United Nations, rather than the Red Army, and to ease up their frantic efforts to build a huge defense industry. The Kremlin might then feel that a further expansion of its security zone is unnecessary, and that it can afford to loosen the lead-strings on its present satellite countries. It might even feel safe in risking some measure of democracy and free speech within its own borders.

But in the meantime we dare not forget the other possibility—that the Soviet bosses may be watching for a chance to spread their doctrine by force of arms. Even if we could somehow be sure that Stalin and his present colleagues in the Politburo have only peaceful intentions, there is no conceivable guarantee that their successors might not be more aggressive. Consequently, until that distant day when a world-wide system of truly collective security can be organized on a basis of mutual trust, we must make certain that we can always defend ourselves against a possible attack from the Soviet half of the world.

That does not, of course, mean merely a defense of our own borders. It means that the present distribution of power, which is now fairly evenly balanced between the Slavs and the Western democracies, must be kept in balance. It means that we cannot permit any expansion of the Soviet community which would eventually give it overwhelming power.

The few simple principles which underlie the defense of this continent have been stated and restated throughout the years by such masters of political geography as Mahan, Spykman, and Lippmann. They are, indeed, so basic and rooted in common sense that anyone who takes the trouble to spend a few hours with a globe and a set of population and resources tables can figure them out for himself. In barest outline, they are:

1. We cannot risk a combination of industrial strength —for example, the linking of Russian industrial centers with the great iron and coal regions of western Germany —which would greatly outweigh our own heavy industry.

2. We cannot let the European seaboard—western Germany, France, the Low Countries, and above all Great Britain—fall under the control of a potentially hostile power, for then command of the Atlantic approaches to our own shores would be irretrievably lost. This elemental strategic fact is understood instinctively by most Americans. Whenever western Europe and the British Isles have been seriously menaced, we have gone to war to protect them—not, at bottom, through any charitable impulse to save these nations, but in our own cold self-interest. Undoubtedly we would do so again. If keeping these areas in friendly hands was vital to our safety in the days of old-fashioned sea power, it is doubly vital in the coming era of guided missiles and ocean-spanning rockets.

3. We cannot permit the vast populations and resources of China and India to slip into the hands of a potential enemy. If that should happen, we would find ourselves, in the long run, hopelessly outmatched, both in manpower and industrial strength.

4. This means that we cannot permit any other nation to build up air-sea power capable of challenging our dominance of the Pacific, or to seize bases on the margins of the Pacific which would serve to develop such air-sea power. Because of this principle and the preceding one, we opposed Japanese expansion in the Pacific to the point of war; they formed the basis of Cordell Hull's so-called

ultimatum which preceded the attack on Pearl Harbor. They are also the foundation of our historic policy— known since John Hay's time as The Open Door—of preserving a united and independent China.

5. No part of the Western Hemisphere, from Patagonia to Greenland, can be yielded to a potentially hostile power. This is the basis of the Monroe Doctrine, a cornerstone of American policy since the infancy of the republic, and of its recent successor, the Act of Chapultepec.

6. Finally, we dare not let a possible enemy get control of certain strategic key points—Iceland, the west coast of Africa, Ascension Island, Gibraltar, the Dardanelles, Salonika, the Persian Gulf, Singapore, Guam, the Aleutians, and perhaps half a dozen others—which could be used as sure steppingstones to conquest of the vital areas already mentioned. That is why we sent a naval force to the Mediterranean as soon as the Russians started putting serious pressure on Greece and Turkey. It is why our marines had to be garrisoned—much to our embarrassment—in North China, and why we had to insist that the Soviets keep their promise to pull out of Iran. That is the reason why we cannot stand aside when the Russians try to make piecemeal advances, no one of which may look, at first glance, particularly serious.

These principles are not the outgrowth of any political theory, nor the property of any one party. They would hold true whether czars or Communists sat in the Kremlin. They would still shape American policy if Germany, Japan, or some other nation were the dominant and expanding force of the Eastern Hemisphere, rather than

Russia. They spring from the unchanging facts of geography and national power, and they will be upheld by whatever party is responsible for our government so long as it has any regard for the long-range security of the American people. We cannot avoid them by an ostrich-like isolationism, nor by clucking a maidenly tongue over the wickedness of "power politics." For power, as Jacques Barzun once remarked, is what politics is all about. Because we have power—more, at the moment, than any other single nation—we cannot escape its politics, nor ignore the principles on which it rests.

The issue, then, is not whether we ought to stand by these principles—in the end, though sometimes tardily, we always do—but how to support them most effectively.

This is not simply a military problem. An adequate army, navy, and air force are essential, of course, along with a network of outlying bases in both oceans; but that is only a beginning. Today a nation's readiness for defense is not measured by the number of men under arms or by the number of planes it can put in the air. It is measured by the ability of its industry to turn out, on short notice, a flood of expensive and complicated machinery. Modern warfare has become, above all else, a problem in industrial engineering.

Consequently, America's future strength will be largely determined by our success in holding our lead both in industrial capacity and in the techniques of production. That means high output—high enough not only to keep our present factories in operation but to stimulate a steady replacement of obsolete plants and equipment. It means a volume of business profitable enough to support heavy investment in scientific research. It means a high demand, with good salaries and steady employment, for our engineers, chemists, and skilled labor. It means, briefly, a healthy, stable economy. *From a strictly military standpoint*, we cannot afford another depression. Nothing else that is likely to happen could shift the balance of military power so disastrously to our disadvantage.

The political balance also depends upon our ability to maintain thriving production and a high level of employment. The economic life of all the western democracies is now meshed tightly with our own, by a web of trade agreements, loans, shipping arrangements, and commodity deals. A depression in this country, therefore, would mean catastrophe for most of our allies. It would spell unemployment and short rations for British factory hands, closed doors for French innkeepers, bankruptcy for Brazilian coffee growers, probably starvation for Bolivian tin miners and Indian jute farmers. It would be a death sentence for democracy throughout wide stretches of the Western community; hungry people notoriously fall easy victims to the infections of either Communism or fascism. If we wanted to hand over the world's vital strategic areas to the Russians, an economic collapse would be the quickest way to do it. They wouldn't have to fire a shot.

If this line of reasoning is correct—and to me it seems self-evident—then it leads to a conclusion already suggested. *The measures which are best calculated to cure Russia's fear neurosis and bring her around to eventual co-operation with the West also are the very measures neces-*

sary to resist Soviet expansion during the intervening period of tension and uncertainty.

On this basis we should be able to build a positive, consistent policy which would take into account both possibilities concerning the Soviet Union's long-range intentions. Such a policy should prove workable, whether Russia's present behavior is merely defensive or whether it turns out to be a prelude to aggression. And it is worth emphasizing once more that the backbone of such a policy must be a prosperous, healthy American economy, freed from the old disastrous cycle of booms and slumps.

In the future, then, United States foreign policy will no longer rest in the hands of Washington. It will depend on the energy, foresight, and responsible behavior of the whole body of American citizens. Every investor, corporation director, and trade union leader will be making foreign policy in the day-to-day handling of his business. And if our economic leaders are really serious in their opposition to Communism, they will waste no time in getting together to figure out means of avoiding another depression. If they let it happen, they not only will ruin themselves; they will betray the whole Western world in the bargain.

If a prosperous economy is the foundation of our foreign policy, it is by no means the whole structure. There are weak spots in our security zone which have to be shored up promptly, if we hope to hold back the creeping tide of Communist expansion. They cannot be stiffened enough merely by sending a few bomber squadrons or visiting warships on a "good-will" mission. What we have to fight here is not Soviet arms but Soviet ideas.

These weak spots are the poverty areas—Greece, the Middle East, China, and the more backward Latin-American countries. They also are the colonial areas. They have long been in economic peonage to Britain or the United States, and in most cases their governments also have been controlled, directly or indirectly, by one or the other of the great capitalist powers.

With their unfailing eye for the main chance, the men in the Kremlin have chosen these areas as their immediate points of attack. For the last two years they have seized every opportunity to pose as the champions of the hungry, hopeless, and oppressed everywhere from Manchuria to Athens. Their propaganda promises a new deal: steady jobs, a burst of economic development, freedom from the old foreign bosses or native feudal rulers—and it points to the remarkable industrial progress of the Soviet Union as proof.

There is only one way we can answer this challenge. We must demonstrate that our system will provide a better living and more freedom than the Communists can offer. If we fail, the poverty areas will be sucked into the Russian orbit sooner or later, in spite of all the military force we can muster. They can be defended only by a democratic revolution, which will sweep away the outmoded colonial regimes and meager peasant economies and which will set up in their place a modern, independent industrial civilization. All the evidence of history (including our own in 1776) goes to prove that such areas cannot be held by force, but that they may be glad to remain as free partners within the Western community, as our own experience with the Philippines has demonstrated.

It happens that most of the danger spots are in the British Empire or, like Greece and the Middle East, within the British sphere of influence. The present Labor government has indicated that it understands—perhaps better than most Americans—what steps are necessary to keep such areas from slipping into Communist control. By its award of independence to India, its withdrawal from Egypt, and its remarkably farsighted plans for reform in colonial administration, it has moved a long way in the right direction.

In her current weakened condition, however, Britain cannot afford either the money or the technicians to put these poverty areas on their economic feet in a hurry. It might prove both sound business and sounder politics for us to lend a hand. We might well supply the capital, the engineers, and the equipment for a Jordan River Authority in Palestine, for example, and a Tigris and Euphrates River Authority in the Arab lands just to the East. (Herbert Hoover, of all people, already has set forth in some detail just how the job could be done.) American machinery and know-how could save twenty years—the crucial twenty years—in the long-overdue industrialization of India and China. And incidentally, programs of this kind, on a really large scale, would take up a lot of the slack when our domestic demand for capital equipment begins to taper off in three or four years.

We would not find such undertakings altogether unfamiliar. During the war we got a good deal of experience with just this sort of task in Latin America. We realized then that only healthy, prosperous democracies, with a rising middle class, could fight off the Nazi virus; and we sent technicians, public-health experts, and farm specialists to the south in droves. We invited Latin Americans to send their own students to the United States for training in every branch of technology (and, on the side, in democracy). We helped build roads, electric power systems, and such basic industries as the new Itabirra steel mill in Brazil. Because the war was absorbing so much of our talent and equipment, this program could not move as fast as some of our Latin-American neighbors wished; but it was a good start—and it worked. It halted the highly dangerous Nazi penetration, and, with the exception of Argentina, a special case, it won the co-operation of all the countries which had been so deeply suspicious of Yankee imperialism a few years earlier. It ought to work equally well against Communist penetration—whether in Latin America, Greece, or China—if it is undertaken on a bold enough scale.

All this will cost money, of course; being a great power never has come cheap. It will provoke grumbling among our more myopic politicians about giving a quart of milk to every Hottentot. But in time, if they are not completely blind, they will come to see that we have to deliver the milk—or the Soviets will. Our economic strength is the greatest single advantage we have in the contest against the Communist half of the world; I am not yet ready to believe that we are fools enough not to use it where it will do the most good.

While we are about it we must remember to avoid one mistake which would be easy—and disastrous—to make. We must never let ourselves be tempted into supporting reactionary ruling cliques simply because they scream loudest against the Communists. Whenever we prop up a Franco in Spain, an Ubico in Latin America, or a corrupt gang of Kuomintang landlords in China, we are betraying our own cause. They may be able to sit on the lid for a few years, but they can never give us the friendship of their people. Our true allies in all of the world's poverty areas are the vigorous progressives, the apostles of democratic revolution. They deserve a good deal more forthright backing than we usually have given them. In China, for example, we could have used our economic aid long ago to force a thoroughgoing reform of the festering Kuomintang dictatorship. A belated sign that we may be learning our lesson was the recent plea of Ambassador John Leighton Stuart for "another internal revolution" against the "selfishly unscrupulous or ignorantly reactionary forces" which have misruled China for so many years.

As we go about the strengthening of the Western democracies, it is important to avoid any action which might inflame Russian suspicion. This will not always be possible. To the conspiratorial and frightened minds of the Soviet rulers, even the most inoffensive behavior sometimes may look like a hostile plot. They undoubtedly interpreted our loan to the British, for instance, as a move toward building up an aggressively anti-Soviet Western bloc; and when the British refused to force General Anders' Polish troops to return home, the Kremlin had nightmares over their possible use as a future emigré army. There are many ways, however, in which we can remove legitimate reasons for Soviet mistrust. A wiser occupation policy, for one thing, ought to demonstrate eventually that we are not trying to preserve the control of reactionary industrialists in Germany and Japan or to set up an anti-Soviet beachhead in Korea. We need to make it clear that we are not backing the fascist remnants in Poland, Rumania, and Hungary who hope that in another war they might regain their feudal privileges. Indeed, it might be well for us to stop meddling altogether in the internal politics of the eastern European puppet states. Because we can't bring predominant power to bear in that area, we cannot change the fundamental character of their governments; and anything short of that accomplishes little except further aggravation of the Communist suspicions. For the same reason, there is not much point in our prolonged refusal to recognize that the Baltic states have been finally merged into the Soviet Union. We could no more restore the independence of Lithuania or Latvia than Russia could restore the independence of Texas. Therefore, we might as well recognize formally that particular fact of life—in return, of course, for an appropriate Soviet concession on other issues.

An early settlement of the German problem obviously

would do more than any other one thing to remove irritants on both sides. No settlement was possible so long as the Soviet bosses thought they had a chance to gobble up the whole country. At the end of the war they undoubtedly expected America to demobilize its armies, pull out of Europe, and go isolationist as it did after World War I— leaving a vacuum in Germany which Russia could move into without much opposition. While that seemed possible, it was simply smart politics for them to stall off any permanent agreement on Germany's future and to keep the country divided and chaotic in hopes that its hungry people would go Communist.

That particular illusion in the mind of the Politburo apparently began to fade when the American people made it plain that they were *not* going isolationist, and that even a return of the Republicans to power would not mean a withdrawal from Europe. Probably it was finally wiped out by Byrnes's Stuttgart speech, re-emphasizing our firm occupation policy and our determination to stand by Western Europe. (Future historians may, indeed, regard that speech as a tide-line, marking the point where the wave of Soviet postwar expansion was finally checked.) Moreover, the German elections in the fall of 1946 and the subsequent crumbling of their pet Socialist Unity Party apparently convinced the Russians that there was no early likelihood of the German people turning to Communism—even in the Soviet zone.

Consequently, at this writing there seems to be some prospect that the Russians finally are ready to talk seriously about negotiating a peace treaty and setting up a unified

German administration under the joint supervision of the Big Four. If that happens, it would probably mean that the Soviets have only temporarily given up their hopes of grabbing control of the whole country for themselves. No doubt they would still figure that the Reich, stripped of most of its industry by bombing and Soviet reparation seizures, eventually would have to turn to Communism as the only way out of its all-but-hopeless economic fix.

Our job would then be to make sure that no such thing happens. Together with England and France, we would have to find some way to avoid the two mistakes we made after the last war. We must keep the Germans permanently disarmed, and at the same time keep them from becoming what Prime Minister Attlee has described as "a cesspool of cheap, underfed, and exploited labor in the middle of Europe," yearning for a dictator to lead them out of their troubles. Apparently these things can be accomplished only by integrating Germany into a democratic, self-supporting federation of Western Europe. That will be a long, hard job; but the only alternative seems to be for American taxpayers to support a pauperized, discontented, and dangerous Germany indefinitely, together with a permanent occupation army to hold it down.

The Russians would not like the idea of a Western European economic and political federation any more than we like the Communist union of Eastern Europe; they would be sure to see in it the fearsome specter of a future anti-Soviet bloc. In the long run they might become reconciled, however, if we and the Western Europeans work together to demonstrate unmistakably that we have no hostile intentions, and that the door is always open for Russian co-operation.

In the military field, Soviet officials feel—as a number of them explained to me—that they have had several legitimate reasons for worry. One of them was the possibility that we might set up permanent bases in Iceland and Okinawa. From these points our bombers might easily wipe out major Soviet industrial centers, including Moscow, Leningrad, and Vladivostok. They are as nervous as we might be if the Russians were able to establish bases (and atomic bombs) on Bermuda and Hawaii.

The withdrawal of our troops from Iceland and our apparent willingness to forego major operational bases on Okinawa and the other Ryukyu islands undoubtedly was a great relief to the Kremlin. And it cost us nothing, since at any serious threat of war we could always grab them first because we hold unchallengable control of both oceans. (A Russian fleet capable of matching our own is something we don't have to worry about for a long time. The Soviet press talks a good deal about building one, but that is a task of twenty years or more, in the present state of Russian technology. Moreover, the Red Fleet must always be kept divided between the Baltic, Arctic, Black, and Pacific waters, which are so situated that concentration is almost impossible. It can never possess the invaluable facility of our navy to assemble all its strength rapidly in either the Atlantic or Pacific by way of the Panama Canal.)

Another cause of Russian worry is the continuation of abnormally large military expenditures in the United States. They see us with a navy greater than all other navies in the world combined; an air force more powerful than all others combined; the only really long-range bombers in the world. Knowing their own temporary weakness, they see no power capable of launching an attack against the United States for years to come. And yet they see us spending more money on armaments than any nation in the world, and far more than we ever before spent in peacetime. *We* know that we have no aggressive intentions; but when other countries look at that bone-crunching military machine, how can they be sure?

Consequently, it may be time for American taxpayers to consider just how much we really need to spend on our military establishment. Nobody can question the necessity of keeping an adequate armed force in readiness; it would be unthinkable to scrap our defenses as we did after World War I. But what is adequate? Is it absolutely necessary to spend for defense eleven billion dollars a year—nearly three times the *total* federal budget in normal pre-depression years?

Nobody knows for sure. Neither the military men who claim they can't get along with a penny less, nor the economy-minded Congressmen who would like to trim off a few billions have yet made a persuasive case. Up to this writing no responsible public body has even inquired in detail how the money would be spent or just where savings might be safely made.

The right level of military expenditure obviously cannot be decided either by unfounded Congressional guesswork or by the unsupported demands of the admirals and generals. (There is no record in history, so far as I know, of any soldier who ever thought he had enough of anything.) Such a question calls for exhaustive study by the best civilian brains we can assemble, sitting as a commission under a Congressional directive to investigate the whole problem of defense policy. A commission of this kind would have to consider: (1) Precisely what commitments must America undertake in each part of the world? (2) How much military strength is necessary to support these commitments? (3) How can such strength be maintained at the lowest possible cost? Until these three questions are settled, a host of minor issues—conscription, for example, and the allocation of funds to the various services—cannot even be debated intelligently. One of the astonishing aspects of American postwar political behavior is our failure to undertake such an inquiry—long advocated by Hanson Baldwin and other military experts—as soon as possible after hostilities ended.

We cannot hope to lighten our armament burden really drastically, of course, until other nations (especially Russia) are willing to disarm at the same time. It is also perfectly plain that no scheme of general disarmament has the slightest chance of working unless it provides for an airtight system of international inspection and control, not only for atomic energy but for all other weapons of mass destruction.

The Soviet bosses are not likely to agree to anything like that for a long time to come. The very thought of permitting a swarm of foreign inspectors—whom they would inevitably regard as spies—to run loose throughout their country is shockingly abhorrent. It collides with that

secrecy obsession which is so deeply rooted both in the
Communists' conspiratorial psychology and in the most
ancient habits of the Russian mind. (The Czarist government was almost as reluctant as Stalin's to let foreigners
cross its borders, and its refusal to honor American passports led to a brisk diplomatic exchange as long ago as
1895.) Moreover, the Soviets don't need international inspectors to tell them what we are doing in arms production;
no doubt American Communists are widely enough dis-
tributed throughout our industry to keep the Kremlin
pretty well informed. We can never entirely prevent such
espionage without suppressing civil liberties and setting up
an NKVD of our own.

In spite of these difficulties, the best we can do is to keep
on trying, with bottomless patience, to persuade the Russians to accept a workable system of disarmament under
international control. There is at least a chance that eventually—once the boundaries between East and West have
become reasonably stabilized—they will come around.
After all, we are offering them a tremendous concession.
Never before in all history has any nation volunteered to
forego a weapon such as atomic energy, which gives it
(for the time being, at least) unquestioned military superiority. And the burden of maintaining large armed
forces strains the Russian economy even more severely
than it does our own.

Meanwhile, do we have any good reason to keep on
manufacturing and stock-piling atomic bombs? If all attempts at international control fail and an atomic arms race
finally becomes unavoidable, our present stock of fission-

able material plus superior technology should insure us an ample lead. Consequently, other nations—not the USSR alone—can see no excuse for our continuing to make bombs just now, unless we have some hidden aggressive purpose at the back of our minds. A suspension of bomb manufacture and a diversion of future uranium production to peaceful uses might go a long way toward easing the atmosphere of tension.

Finally, in our day-to-day dealings with the Russians we need to learn an almost superhuman forbearance and tact. Unquestionably they are the most irritating negotiators since Genghis Khan. Even so forgiving a soul as Mrs. Roosevelt was moved to describe her work with them on the UN Economic and Social Council as "the most exasperating thing in the world." They think nothing of making outrageous demands which they know cannot be granted, of ignoring all their opponents' arguments, of insulting their one-time allies with remarks such as Vishinsky's "while our blood flowed, you were making profits." A Soviet representative in Washington once told an UNRRA colleague of mine who had had considerable diplomatic experience that he was not important enough to go on a mission to Russia; and insinuations that Western statesmen do not really represent their people are a standard gambit in Communist tactics.

In part, such manners are a deliberate effort to get under our skin, and therefore should be ignored. But they are also, in part, a natural outgrowth of Russian history and Communist dogma. Soviet spokesmen can't help acting that way, any more than Mr. Truman can stop talking with a Missouri accent, and to the extent this is true, their behavior should be forgiven.

We must remember that they are Orientals with the same bargaining instincts as an Armenian rug dealer. To them it is normal to start out with an asking price ten times as high as the price they finally expect to close for. They also expect the customer to walk out the door a few times while the haggling is going on. (I ran onto one incident in Russian history where the czar's envoys were instructed, on pain of death, not to yield a single inch until the Polish ambassador broke off the conference and rode away in his sleigh. Then they were to gallop after him and offer a small concession to persuade him to return to the parley.) They simply can't understand our taking offense at such tactics, and they can't believe us when we say that we cannot recede from a position taken at the beginning of negotiations.

We should remember, too, that the Soviet Union is a young nation which has been through terrible experiences during its short life. Consequently, its spokesmen reflect all of the national shyness, uncertainty, and inexperience. Is it so strange, after all, that they should act like an awkward adolescent (long treated as a pariah) who is invited to his first party? In the pinfeather stage of our republic, Americans, too, exhibited a good deal of blatant self-assertiveness. It is simply what Mrs. Roosevelt characterized as "the arrogance of insecurity."

Moreover, every Russian abroad believes profoundly that he is dealing with the heathen. In his mind is a myth of The Evil Capitalist—a sly fellow, his checkbook always primed for bribery, who breakfasts on children of the downtrodden worker and plots incessantly against the Soviet people. It is a picture not much further from reality than the image of the Bolshevik—a bearded madman with bombs in each hand—which is still cherished by some of our stuffier conservatives. The main difference is that the Russian's myth is ground into his head by all the pressure of official propaganda, and he has no chance to correct it by unbiased study. Consequently, he treats all foreigners as if they were about to pick his pocket or assault his virtue.

This invincible misunderstanding of the outside world is largely responsible for Russia's bad public relations. The Communists regard foreign correspondents in Moscow both as potential spies and as capitalist hirelings who are under orders to smear the Soviet Union. (In a few cases the latter has been all too true, but it is, of course, not true of the majority of Moscow correspondents.) As a result, the Russians treat visiting newspapermen with thinly veiled contempt, and keep them penned as closely as possible in the Metropole Hotel. There the correspondents get stir-crazy, and often become unduly embittered toward their Soviet jailers.

In fact, the whole idea of objective reporting is beyond the Russian's comprehension. The well-trained Communist believes, in the words of *Pravda*, that journalism—whether capitalist or Soviet—"cannot be nonpolitical." He does not greatly respect objective truth, even as an ideal; to him the value of any statement is not measured by its correspondence to fact but by its effect on the minds of men. And this state of mind applies to Communist diplomacy just as it does to Communist journalism.

In like manner, the Russian notion of an agreement is very different from our own. Apparently a bargain with the Soviets can be managed successfully only on the basis of simultaneous delivery. Whenever we carry through our part of the deal first, they seem to have no compunction about wriggling out of their half. At best, they try to sell everything twice—getting one concession when they agree to do something "in principle" and then demanding another before they will execute the agreement. Thus they agreed at Potsdam to the economic unification of Germany; and within a few months they were demanding astronomical deliveries of reparations from the Western zones as an extra payment for putting the unification into effect. Similarly, they began to run out on their Yalta commitments within a few weeks after the papers were signed, and they have repeatedly ignored our requests that they settle up their lend-lease bills. In their code of morality, all this presumably is regarded as a laudable outwitting of the rascally foreigner.

The technique of Soviet diplomacy might, indeed, be described as a mixture of the Byzantine and the Marxist conspiratorial traditions. It is compounded of force, threats, deceit, secrecy, and complex intrigue. Even Soviet ambassadors are never trusted on a very long leash; they can make no important move, concession, or statement without Politburo clearance. The notion that any man could loyally serve an international organization—UNRRA or the United Nations—rather than his own state is utterly foreign to the Russian mind. For example, some Soviet officials apparently never were convinced that our mission was not reporting constantly to the American embassy in Moscow, rather than to UNRRA headquarters alone.

Such people obviously are going to be difficult to get along with; but we must learn to do it, with all the tolerance and patience we can muster. The American diplomat whose opinion on Russian affairs I value most once privately summed up the problem in these terms:

"We can contribute only by a long-term policy of firmness, patience, and understanding, designed to keep the Russians confronted with superior strength at every juncture where they might otherwise be inclined to encroach upon the vital interests of a stable and peaceful world; but we should do this in so friendly and unprovocative a manner that its basic purposes will not be subject to misinterpretation."

Four or five years from now the division of the world between the Communists and the Western democracies probably will be fairly well completed. The dividing line —now in dispute in such trouble spots as Germany, the Middle East, and China—may have become reasonably distinct and firm. We may then find a more stable world than these gloomy and turbulent times lead us to expect. These seem likely to be its salient characteristics:

1. For the first time the world will be organized into two great power systems, instead of being split among seven or more major powers and dozens of little ones.

Consequently, it might be expected to prove a more solid type of organization. So long as there were several Great Powers, all roughly comparable in strength, there existed an almost infinite opportunity for intrigue and combination. Every nation had to be perpetually uneasy about what its neighbors were doing; they might gang up at any moment. And in real or imagined self-defense, each sought to improve its own network of shifting alliances. In the future there clearly will be far less room for this sort of dangerous maneuver.

2. For the first time the two greatest powers will be widely separated, rather than face to face across a fortified border or narrow seas. War between them would appear to be less likely, simply because either one would find it almost impossible to reach the vital centers of the other. The atom bomb and long-range guided missiles will not change this fact. We and the Russians might destroy each other's cities in an atomic cataclysm, but neither could gain decisive victory without occupying the territory of the other. For reasons noted below, neither would be likely to find that possible.

3. The nature of the military strength of the two Super-Powers is entirely different. America is primarily an air-sea power; Russia a land power. An American general staff could hardly contemplate an invasion of the vast land masses of the Soviet Union, in the face of Russia's incomparably greater resources in military manpower. (This disparity will continue to grow. Long-term population trends will give Russia a sharply increasing proportion of its people within the military age brackets, while the proportion

of Americans of military age will decrease.) Conversely, Russia—which has no navy of consequence and will not have in our time—could hardly land an army on our shores in the face of the American fleet, regardless of atom bombs on both sides. As Lippmann has suggested, an outright military struggle between the two would be almost as improbable as a fight between an elephant and a whale.

4. Within both Russia and the United States, certain internal factors will tend to discourage a warlike policy for years to come. In Russia the memory of the tremendous casualties of World War II will serve as an inhibiting influence for at least a generation; and it may well be that long before Soviet industry is fit to wage another war. In the United States, the traditional antiwar sentiment will be reinforced by the towering public debt, a swarm of domestic economic problems, and the approaching exhaustion of certain strategic raw materials—notably high-grade iron ore, bauxite, copper, and oil.

5. Finally—as Hanson Baldwin and other military students have pointed out—there is no fundamental strategic conflict between Russia and the United States. Each can build an adequate structure of regional security without threatening the other. After the boundary between the two orbits becomes clear and fixed, a major war could occur only if one of the great regional systems mounted a deliberate, full-scale attack on the other. Such an attack—from either side—would be very difficult to organize, and its chances of success would be small. Moreover, for the first time in history, neither side could hope to profit from a quick, cheap victory. Atomic retaliation would be quick

and ruinous; there can no longer be any doubt that war would be a disaster for victor and vanquished alike.

Once the present grinding adjustments to the new two-power arrangement have been completed, therefore, we might reasonably look forward to a considerable period of stability. It would hardly be accurate to call it peace; it will more nearly resemble an armed truce. But if the balance can be held even, if the Western half of the world can remain prosperous, strong, and democratic—then over the course of years the men in the Kremlin may get over their fearfulness and mistrust. And eventually—perhaps in another generation—the truce may be converted into peace.